HOME FRONT

HOME FRONT

BRYONY DORAN • BULLETPROOF
JEHANNE DUBROW • STATESIDE
ELYSE FENTON • CLAMOR
ISABEL PALMER • ATMOSPHERICS

BLOODAXE BOOKS

ISBN: 978 1 78037 326 3

First published 2016 by
Bloodaxe Books Ltd,
Eastburn,
South Park,
Hexham,
Northumberland NE46 1BS.

www.bloodaxebooks.com
For further information about Bloodaxe titles
please visit our website or write to
the above address for a catalogue.

Supported using public funding by
ARTS COUNCIL
ENGLAND

44670
c(23.11.16)

Cover design: Neil Astley & Pamela Robertson-Pearce.

Printed in Great Britain by Bell & Bain Limited, Glasgow, Scotland, on
acid-free paper sourced from mills with FSC chain of custody certification.

ACKNOWLEDGEMENTS

Jehanne Dubrow's *Stateside* was first published by Northwestern University Press in its Triquarterly Books imprint in 2010, with a foreword by Ted Kooser. Elyse Fenton's *Clamor* won Cleveland State University Poetry Center's First Book Prize selected by D.A. Powell, and was published in the CSU Poetry Series in 2010, winning the 2010 University of Wales Dylan Thomas Prize despite the book not being published in the UK. Bryony Doran's *Bulletproof* and Isabel Palmer's *Atmospherics* are first published in *Home Front*, as are their forewords by Ruth Padel and Andrew Motion. Rachel Zucker's foreword to *Clamor* in this edition was first published in 2011 in the Poetry Society of America's New American Poets series on www.poetrysociety.org

Some of the poems in *Atmospherics* were included in *Ground Signs* (Flarestack Poets, 2014), a Poetry Book Society Pamphlet Choice; some originally appeared in *The Frogmore Papers*, *The North* and *Stand*, and some were read by Isabel Palmer on BBC Wiltshire and on Radio 4's *The World at One with Martha Kearney*. Bryony Doran's poem 'Floods in Queensland' first appeared in the anthology *Millstone Grit*, as part of Sheffield Hallam University's Catalyst project.

CONTENTS

III

ISABEL PALMER

ATMOSPHERICS

(2016)

ATMOSPHERICS

The narrative in Isabel Palmer's *Atmospherics* begins with seeing her only son go to war in Afghanistan soon after his 21st birthday in 2011 in 2011, and ends after his final, safe return. His role there was to lead foot patrols and to operate machines for detecting improvised explosive devices. While he was on tour, she wrote one poem every week reflecting on their experiences.

Isabel Palmer is a freelance writer and a former English teacher and educational adviser. She lives in Swindon. Her pamphlet, *Ground Signs* (Flarestack Poets, 2014), was a Poetry Book Society Pamphlet Choice. In 2015 she read some of the poems on BBC Wiltshire and on Radio 4's *The World at One with Martha Kearney*, gave readings at the States of Independence event at De Montfort University, Leicester, and at Swindon Poetry Festival, and had a residency at Marlborough College. Her first full-length collection, *Atmospherics*, is first published here in *Home Front*. Her father and her son both served in the Rifles.

FOREWORD

As military conflicts drag on into the 21st century, we're gradually becoming used to the idea that war poetry comes in more various shapes and sizes than many people thought a generation or two ago. In the 1960s and 70s, as the reputations of the great British poets of the First World War started to thrive (boosted in part by their beginning to appear as a regular feature on school curricula), it was commonly assumed that their way was the only way to do things. War poetry, that's to say, meant traumatised men keeping close contact with one another ('I am the enemy you killed, my friend') in a hideously mangled landscape of mud and wire. Poets of the Second World War, even the marvellous Keith Douglas, have never received the same kind of attention or praise, partly because they don't conform to this pattern. (Douglas sees his enemy in 'a dial of glass' – at a heart-chilling remove.) And as for women poets (whether they were writing as nurses, or as girlfriend or sisters or wives or mothers), or poets of the home front... By and large, they had to make do with shady corners of the anthologies, when they were not ignored altogether.

These days, we're almost startled to come across first-hand accounts of the front line in collections about contemporary wars. In their place we find poems derived from interviews or current affairs programmes, or with other kinds of oversight and reaction from behind the lines. The benefits can be significant: a proof of deep sympathy in a wide range of voices. The danger, of course, is that however well-meant they might be, they will seem opportunistic – a parading of sensitivity that exists at a damaging distance from its ostensible subject.

No such problem affects these poems by Isabel Palmer: as the mother of a soldier, the sincerity of her feeling is never in doubt, but this has less to do with the feelings themselves than her skill as a writer. Whether she's talking about her son in Helmand or her son at home, herself in his company or her self alone, she never takes her eye off things in themselves. Some of these details are familiar and domestic, some are faraway and strange. Some exist in a kind of pure isolation, some are jumbled together so that scenes of peace and scenes of war become convincingly and troublingly combined. All serve as the starting-point of powerful emotions, but are also the anchors for those emotions – so that extreme states become at once particular and general.

This is what makes *Atmospherics* such a rewarding collection. Its subjects have a high level of documentary interest, but Isabel Palmer's particular achievement is to invest them with the authority of the heart. She shows us the danger and distress of conflict from an angle that is unusual in poetry, while reminding us that her point of view is ancient as warfare itself.

ANDREW MOTION

ATMOSPHERICS

Home

8TH AUGUST – 9TH OCTOBER 2011

Worst Case Scenario

Pre-deployment family briefing: Rifles HQ, London

The Captain didn't say why
he would only loiter at the gate
if bad news comes calling.

Someone will come up your garden path –
it won't be me –
within two hours
and they'll stay with you.

He didn't say how long
or why there would be two of them
when one sorry magpie could do the job

or what use they'd be to someone
who knows everywhere you've been,
can look at a map of anywhere
and see only the shape of you –
how you can move
like a mantis, praying,
that rocks and ratchets
along a swaying leaf.

But when he asked for questions,
I was thinking, *Why*
do they have to iron uniforms
to go out on patrol?

As if smoothness could keep you safer
than all the browns and yellows in the world,
or heat could stroke the breath
into a tunic's body
to keep the bullets out.

So when I said, *If they must*
come, don't make it on a Tuesday –
I have Ellie then,

he didn't write it down.

Portrait

If you're reading this
is too morbid, you say, a photograph
will do. I want more.

A portrait in oils, slow
enough to think itself dry, each layer
of colour with time to change

its mind. A likeness close enough
to get you arrested, the brush knowing
its way around the square

of your chin, your lower lip buttered
with light. Shadows behind
and around, Klein blue, the young man's

share of the world, the sky's deeds
signed; blue too fine
to wear, stretched across

mountains, deserts, oceans,
our own planet rising, sea-sparkled,
above the Moon's horizon.

Whatever

I meant to say
whatever you did
was fine by me but I didn't
and it wasn't.

I was wrong or
you were
but something right came of it
and out of you
though I can't tell now
if that was
inside me or out.

The memory is there
of a journey to another time;
you and I returned changed,
our lives spelt differently,
one letter at a time.

Now whatever it was
would take a nesting blackbird
the ultraviolet
of her chick's gaping throat
to see.

I couldn't find the words
if someone jammed a screwdriver
down my throat to twist out
my swallowed tongue.

You've got to call it something

Your grandfather called her Ellen, his first one,
after his mother and that was why maybe
he had a hard time killing, though she was
fast and sleek as a salmon

and why he kept her primed
and polished through the war
and the peace at each side.

But what I remember is a midsummer's evening
and that policeman, *You have to have a licence, sir,*
or surrender your firearms and the noise his throat made
as he broke her back on the old vice.

So, if yours must have a name, make it
Alpha, Lima or Sierra, or the Bond girl glamour
of Pussy, Domino or Dr Warmflash –

no saint's name to take in vain
or Shakespeare's army of martyred women
but a name without formal ceremony
like a guest you can let go
without longing.

Hey Diddle Diddle

For you the soaring melody, the virtuoso
flourishes: his name, birthday, regiment, my answer
on the lower strings, the girl in me at last

not minding. For I know what it is
to play second fiddle to a cat,
a cow, a thin slice of moon, so low

the night I was born, you could hurdle
it, though the cat was shot in Moccas Park
and the cow hadn't jumped since

he sold her calf at Ludlow Market. Still
I had no name or number,
though cow and calf had both –

R3065 (1 and 2), Dawn and Dumbo
when they licked his hand
at the orchard gate, their spit thick

as new paint on my old pram. Yet,
he could name a wish of snipe, a charm
of goldfinches, grists, bazaars, whole looms

of bees, guillemots, camels, shoot
five rabbits at the white wall,
a dish fit for a queen, knit dreams

of Jeannie with the light-brown hair
without dropping a stitch, give odds
on picking eight score-draws in one line

of seventy-eight billion to one
and, laughing, toast the early rising
Dog Star and his pup,

while nurses fed me
spoonfuls of air as thick
as silver plate.

Ground Signs

'Why you?'
Not so long ago,
you could lose
keys, batteries, bicycles and limp
home with just one shoe.

'Is there no one else? One
who can drop on his belt buckle
at a sudden shrine
of painted stones: red,
white, *surkh*, *safayd*. Someone

who knows better than to cross a ditch
no wider, on the landing side,
than one soldier's boot,

who sifts the ground signs ankle-deep
in upturned soil, still fresh
in midday sun, at slow-down points
of overlooking, who notes

the shifting sand on wood and track,
the locals out of sight,

the old man's goat left bleeding.

Someone to keep a steady hand and eye,
who tilts the Vallon's search-head,
ear to the ground, sweeping
for the metal spoor
of battery pack and detonator wire.

'Who could stop you then?'

No woman who waits,
picking, unpicking,

not Odysseus himself, lifted
from that rock of road.

The Story's Fault

I blame the stories. *Flat Stanley*, crushed
by a bulletin board, like clothes
waiting for a holiday.

Though they blew him up
with a bicycle-pump until
his buttons burst, always
one part stayed flat.

You had your dad
put up a board that covered
the whole wall and waited
for it to fall on you.

Are waiting still.

The Snow Queen too, splinters
in hearts and minds, each grain of sand
with the power of the whole desert
when it gets in your boots; *Thomas*

the Tank with his human face and *Tootle*,
straying from the tracks when all it took
was locals waving red flags, no wolves,
no bellies filled with stones,
to make him forget
he ever loved flowers.

And Jack, the beanstalk
tall as poppies, his mother running
to fetch the axe she could never use.

The one that you forgot: *Swiss Family Robinson*,
no miracles to be made, where a jackal's
as harmless as a treehouse
lined with books, where no one

ever

gets up, puts on his coat.

The Watch

Bristol Airport: 9th October 2011

If what you want most in the world
is for time to run backwards,
it will cost you twelve pounds,
more if you want the stopwatch function

or the second hour hand for the badlands
of Nahr-e Saraj, Alikozai, Babaji,
where time is both ahead and behind,
its face turned backwards
in the eighth circle of Hell.

Because that's not how it rolls with soldiers,
you'll have no rose gold or platinum,
quartz or battery but steel
and weights, cogs and gears
to make a man of you,

with your whole life
and all the lives you could have,
beginning with those same eyes,
that wide-mouthed smile –

a watch to tell the days backwards
to the point of ordnance,
that last airport parting,
18.07.41 local time,

with no safe crash landing,
no jury-rigging genius
or free return trajectory,
then or now, only

the slow tilt of your jaw
to the shadow side of a kiss

like the mid-course correction burn,
fourteen seconds, no more or less,
that brought Apollo 13 home.

Helmand Province, Afghanistan

MONDAY, 17TH OCTOBER 2011 – WEDNESDAY, 25TH APRIL 2012

Glossolalia

Helmand: 17th October 2011

There was a time when old men in church
whispered prayers into their hats
so only God could hear

or spoke in tongues, a scat
chorus of word noise, syllables spread,
waiting to be searched.

Once tight-lipped boys tongued
the order to advance, to skirmish or retreat,
shook the air awake with silver bugles.

Now *Fuck, incoming!* shrieks
between lip and teeth, *Allahu Akbar*
on the radio like a child talking backwards.

Man down! snaps the jaws
of a roadside bomb. A boot
makes bloody footprints
on a nest of cloud.

The sniper's bullet snags the air
with the sand lark's rise and fall, singing
to its last wing beat.

Someone's prayer rocks
a cradle of branches, riffs
with the wind, *shu-ah, shu-ah, shu-ah,*
as the world falls.

Blueprint

The TV ad ran for forty seconds
and five years, saved who knows
how many children

from going lame. Just
a child's foot, an adult hand,
a blue felt-tip with five

points of contact: toes,
ball, arch, instep, heel, to show
how the little foot will grow,

the sturdy buckle fastened
on the second hole, attentive
and exact as love. A blueprint

for what comes after: a medic
with a blue felt-tip, a squaddie volunteer,
stripped to his shorts, five points

of contact. A line above the knees
to show how blast fragments travel
upwards, through genitals

and heart, how the rifle bounces,
shatters jaw, teeth, skull, no one
rushing out to put the kettle on.

Honour Guard

I knew we were in trouble
when you started putting x

on every message
as though your time was coming and going now
in dog years.

But it was still a shock between
Watchfield and Swindon,
outside the new police station, Adele on the radio,

when all I was ready for
were traffic lights,
a tantrum at roadworks

and there they were –
cars growling at a rope of police cars,
flowers thrown

like the flax
that mothers, fathers, sisters
gave dry-eyed little witch girls
to make them burn faster,
to get it over with.

That Time

So even here's a warzone,
334 steps winding up
Big Ben's tower,

brick, stone, iron,
bare-knuckled against
the fountains of excited atoms, laser-cooled
in crystal oscillation,
in the latest speaking clock.

Making do and mending
where time and timing matters most,
with only pennies on the pendulum to balance,
two-fifths of a second perfect.

You on look-out, a sangar of sandbags, rocks,
camouflage, firing your GPMG
with one eye closed.

Even with a face
on all four sides,
mistakes are made –

one pane of glass pink

not following the rules, like him,
stepping off the path you marked
to take a piss.

Men risk life and limb
in tight formation
to abseil down, to clear and hold
insurgent grime,
dodging the gun metal hand
that fires at one o' clock.

Wall rungs, for the old
gas lighter, that Jack
would need his beanstalk legs
to climb,

disappear oddly
into air above,
and that cracked giant bell,
at first a background warbling
in E natural, G sharp, F sharp, E and B

All through this hour, Lord be my Guide. And
by thy power, no foot shall slide

astride that ditch, the landing safe
but one foot slipping back

exploding in our ears,

far too close,

ringing, ringing, ringing.

Language Card (Dari)

There are not more than five primary colours, yet in
combination they produce more hues than ever can be seen.

SUN TZU, *The Art of War*, *c.* 550 BC

On the cover, they are neither flesh
nor blood, the blue burka draped
in unwomanly folds. The boy
with hair like moulded plastic salutes,
palm downwards, the American way,
as though his hands were dirty.

Questions hang violet in colour space, step
from shadows, smiling; child, bomber, thief
the same shade of pink, time itself
poisonous yellow that lingers
on your fingertips.

Orders are red: cars spinning
on a bend, stilettos dancing on tables,
blood. There are no words
for fog, flood, scorch, only the slow
shift towards tomorrow *fardaa*, next month,
maa-ay aayenda, when every day but one
is Saturday or a sparkling imitation: *shambay*,
yakshambay, *dushambay*, the wire cage uncorked,
nails, ball-bearings, human dung.

Small talk is green, pale enough
to rub out with one finger, *salaam alaykum*
flicked overhead like a scorpion's tail, while grenades
rockets, mortars, grey as old crows,
peck skin-winged clouds, shred sky
and silence.

Last, a cross-hatching of tones, light
to dark green for body parts, *soukhta*
for how bones melt; one word, *dest*
for the arm that's lost and the hand
that took it. Only in Pashto, two words, *baazu, laas,*
line up against a compound wall,
hands on their heads.

BFPO

You ask for fifty pounds
for boots: second-hand, worn in, broad
as camel feet, to roll away dust
like a third eyelid. I speak wishes,
drop silver into wells.

You long for body spray, manly vetivers,
heavy as church windows, of smoky leather
and cigars, stronger than your
greenhouse air when poppies lean
their heads against stained skies. I send
cool crystals to grow snowmen, mistletoe,
Christmas trees.

You want magazines with cars, workouts,
gizmos and photographs of Rio girls
whose skin must smell of oranges
and limes. I send you Windsor Castle,
Westminster, Big Ben, Churchill's beaches,
sunny uplands, speeches and *I vow to thee,
my country, all earthly things above*
on postcards.

So, when you ask me what can mend
the pulsing in your ears, the mousetrap snap
of each grenade, the rifle's nibbling
echoes of the nearest bullet yet,
I send you cheese, beef jerky, protein bars

and think this must be how it feels
to be looking at a rainbow as a child
steps in front of a car.

Boots

It was the day that Afghan soldier stole your boots
and I was down to my last shoebox, even though
Cathy had brought round twenty, the week before,
when everyone in the queue in Shoe City gave her
theirs and wore their new shoes home even though it
was raining and some had strappy sandals.
There it was, just as I'd sent it – except for the angry
sticker, the mention of dangerous items –
the parcel I'd sent: plastic boxes with airtight lids
to keep out mice with a taste for protein bars, chilli-
flavoured biltong, washing line, plastic pegs
and the Babybel from the trip to Calais
with the Welfare Team.   No prohibited items:
aerosols, lighters, alcohol – when Baz's gran sent port
that was only found when he tried
to smuggle it back through Brize when he came home
on R and R and Mark sewed live rounds
in his pockets for a joke – nothing at all to offend
cultural values, not even the model
on the cover of *Men's Health* when there were
dozens like him in every patrol base to see first-hand,
not the Barbie Princess cups, KFC wrappers
or the cider-making kit full of Pringles; not even
the Smurfs colouring-book, the Afghan
Commander checking you kept inside the lines

                         and you said
what a pity you wouldn't get the chance,
when you caught the guy who pinched
your boots, to string him up with washing line,
force-feed him cheese and
throw him a Tupperware party.

R and R

Wiltshire, 25th February 2012

No one was looking when the sky fell
on Fukushima, as the sun
tore off her colours and flung
them in the sea. Only Mr Yoshizawa

saw cars bounce, buildings bend
like willow sticks, watched at dawn
as fishermen shot their lines, a rebel *feu de joie*
at poisoned seas. For weeks

he lived on biscuits, dry as the herbs
the hare sits pounding in the moon,
dreaming of oysters, froth of jade
on hot, sweet tea, matsutake broth.

Night and day he worked, like the wagtail
that beat the waters back, made safe
the land for men to hunt and fish.

Later, on a Tokyo train going home,
like Aioina shunned in heaven
for his human clothes, he sat alone though
travellers overlapped, tight
as turtles. Like you,

on leave from Helmand, on the Tube,
your carriage corner brightly lit,
the dark outside,
your face a floating moon,
with a stare
any hand could pass
straight through.

Zia

We must have played it a hundred times,
re-arranging the Furniture Game, checking
behind the sofa for the lost metaphor.
If he was a weapon, what weapon would he be?

Some kind of sword.
At twelve, he didn't know the word, in Pashto
or English but it took off his mother's head
as they stretched his eyelids open.

If you were a Shakespeare play, which play would you be?

'*Romeo and Juliet.*' Although it was the first
and only one he knew. *Beautiful Juliet,*
thus from my lips by thine,
my sin is purged.

May and the quarrel starts again,
after the harvest
and we're reading Zia's coursework,
our tears running off like poppy milk,

If the man was an item of footwear, what
item of footwear would he be?

Flip flops looking for their feet
outside a blown-up army base.

Absent Fathers

To get to the top, they say,
it helps if you've been abandoned
by one parent or another. Not having a father

leaves room for you to make your own,
Blue Peter-style, from an Apache pilot
and the winner of the Tour de France.

They say it's harder on boys
who'll only take orders
from someone who can run a mile

in six minutes or less, take
a bearing from the horns
of a crescent moon

and silence a boy with a downturn in his voice,
secret as a dog's whistle.

Easter Assembly

The hand that holds the paper
has no pity for its emptiness,
its plain white shrouding. It waits

for stillness, can turn
a single page into swords, clubs,
vinegar and thorns. They need

proof: a show of back
and front, top
and bottom, demand to see

the nails in the hands,
the naked blood-sweat,
the 'Who hit you, Prophet?'

blindfold game.
He's too good, his secret
to keep his head still, eyes fixed

as his fingers work, like a pigeon's
rhythmic flick between one step
and the next. He rocks

his fist across the creases, cuts
the paper into two to make
a cross that flies, the shape

of Christ, long-limbed
across his mother's knees,
with a flick of the wrist,
lets God go.

Chaos Theory

An old man in the basket-only queue at M & S
with Ellie in her pink ruffled frock and red shoes
tugging against gravity,
restless as a spinning moon.

What kind of man buys only chocolate
in shapes of baby animals, when
it's not Christmas or Easter,
just a soggy braincloud
of an April day?

We couldn't look at him
though the rabbit was already
missing its head
but the flutter of a thank you flashed
its violet warning like a wing.

And faraway in your world,
with the air swinging dry
on a mother's bowed head,
her back turned against you.
Her son speaks for her,
as he must for all our sakes,
salaam alaykum, tashakur
as you reach for the chocolate
you always carry, though it's 42 degrees
and your Bergen has peeled
the skin from your shoulders.

He's talking fast, *enfejaar, enfejaar,*
pointing, *da chaar tarafay,*
da chaar tarafay,
away from where the big thing is until
you make the slightest change of course,
like a number rounded off

or a child's wobbly scissor work,
outside the lines, the tiny perturbation
that can make tornadoes
from a spinning cloud.

Gold

(After seeing the British Museum's Exhibition of Bactrian Gold entitled 'Afghanistan: Crossroads of the Ancient World')

Who would have thought that anyone
could make a golden cape, four metres long
from spider silk? A million spiders

harnessed for early morning silking, bellies
stroked until gold spills, threads curdled
into shawls, chasubles, orphreys,
tattooed with spiderlings. Who knew

that in a Kabul vault, spinnarets
like enormous thumbs would spin dust
to gold, stronger than combat vests, that

a rich man's nomad bones could turn
to gold in Tillya Tepe's threadbare
light, make rings, necklaces, a light show
of suns streaming from a crown

that folds, like goshawk wings,
inside a saddle-bag, that gems
could paint such muscles on a horse,
his eyeballs marbled with agate, garnet

swelling at his neck, that turquoise
could check the tide-pull of his flight
with stolen deep-sea sunlight?

Who would have thought
that holders of the treasure keys would keep
the secret of their names tight
as limpet teeth, the life of every newborn
hanging by a thread?

Homecoming

HOMER: 'What's an email?'
LENNY: 'It's a computer thing, like, er, an electric letter.'
CARL: 'Or a quiet phone call.'

The Simpsons (Fox TV)

18th April 2012 15:54

Flights will be between 27 and 30 April... Odd individuals may fall outside those dates. We expect you on the 26th.

19th April 2012 16:12

He says you're *inbound*. Then, you're *on the boat*, to be delivered to RTMC Chilwell tomorrow, as expected, like a gift there is no time to wrap. He doesn't say if the sea is rough, whether you have medicine for sea sickness, that provision has been made for the sudden change in temperature.

He calls us *Dear Families* as though he would like to shake our hands, though personal responses are not expected. He is careful to use the same subject description every time: *Release-authorised: Rifles Return*. Electronic filters require exact matches.

He builds a bridgehead: no line more than eighty characters, the body of the message never deeper than sixteen lines. It is impossible to know if smallsteps2101769@sky.com is mother, father, partner, brother but chances are that elevendartfinish@yahoo.co.uk is male and that rainbowglitterfairy@btinternet.com is a young wife or girl-friend and may have small children.

25th April 2012 17:26

No record exists of how many times recipients checked their emails in the hours before dawn and after dusk. The screen tells them they have been signed in for 7 days, 1 hour and 32 minutes. This is not the time to flick days aside like beads on an abacus, not the place for ribbons and bows, for renewing rapport with *You see* or *you know* and, at the mention of Cyprus, for smileys wearing sunglasses. The modalities are different, the tone required hushed and monastic, like David Attenborough stalking young lions.

Collecting soldiers in person will entail extra fuel costs, sitting in traffic and of course waiting...

Home

THURSDAY, 26TH APRIL 2012 – FRIDAY, 13TH MARCH 2015

Signs

2 Rifles, Ballykinler, N. Ireland: 15th May 2012

Things that mean other things: tattoos, cap badges,
padlocks on lampposts, on garbage bins,
along the *Ponte Milvio*.

An old man in a field, folded
like a sleeping bird, a farmer digging
by moonlight; wheat, maize, poppies
shoulder-high, a draped flag of sky.

Other things: clay bricks, an unsmoked cigar
beneath a wooden cross, a branch
tied to a donkey's tail; a boy

who stands too long
on the cross-hairs of a passing convoy;
mirror flashes, kites that hang
on days of rising wind, their feet swaying.

A mulberry grove in a frontline checkpoint,
a stream that spins its silk cocoon
slowly, afraid to go outside.

So when you see
that squaddie who lost his legs,
whose fingers, on his rifle hand, clung
to his elbow like scorched fruit,

on his way to the Medals Parade,
his laughter rattling like old bones,
you have to look away.

Symbols

1 *Mathematical*

A footprint of buried wire

$+$

plastic bags, bottles, tyres
too good to throw away, sand
on roadsides, mobiles, white
pellets, nitrogen 35% proof
like a shot of bootleg brandy

$-$

cars, pick-ups, children

$\times$

foot patrols, mouseholes
entry points cleared,
ladders that lean against
compound walls balance
on their fingertips

$=$

454

at last count. Each day

$\div$

sun, moon, stars
like too many pips
on dice already rolled. Five,

ten fighters at the tree-line,
leaves that drop from widow branches,
shouting, finger talk,

all Euclid's calculations
proved at the point of a compass,
a straight line of dust. Counting

on fingers, toes, elbows: £140,000
for the lost chin, nose, lip, the taste
of old lives; £27,000 for a thumb,

index finger, the use
of one foot, for empty levels
in your stack of bones.

Symbols

2 *Pictorial*

T for tourniquet and time
written somewhere visible,
for bleeding, breaks, burns
with rollaway skin. M for morphine,

press and hold, one to ten, the end
against the upper thigh purple,
the colour of explosives,
home-made, strip-searched.

A game of *Operation*, tweezers,
body parts, flimsy plastic, broken
wires, helicopters that nudge the sides
of battlefields, buzzing, noses flashing.

Tin Can alley, pop-up
fighters from holes
in compound walls, rifle-fire
flashing red, short of target.

A *Tonka* tank of cold-rolled steel,
Action Man on the dashboard, sent
from home in sniper pose
right side up – though he

couldn't stand anyway
on grass or sand – with gripping
hands and battle-scars
from afternoons spent

tied to chairs, from penknife
eviscerations, smotherings
by scarves, hand-knitted
and motherly.

Symbols

3 *Linguistic*

> *Ventriloquism: n.* act or art of speaking or uttering sounds in such a manner that the voice appears to come from some source other than the speaker (L. *venter,* belly; *loqui,* speak).

> *Field: n & v* 1. *n* (piece of) ground, esp. one used for pasture or tillage; 2. ground for playing cricket, football, etc; 3. ground on which battle is fought, battlefield; **a fair field and no favour:** equal conditions in contest; *field dressing* (wet): for phosphorus burns, protruding organs.

Someone has stolen
your voice, his hand
on your back, speaking
of *lizards* and *seagull*
colonels without moving
his lips, spitting like troll
water in a flooded ditch, *sierra,*
tango, foxtrot, uniform: snakes
that strike with all
their parts: head, tail,
crushing abdominals

and no one speaks of fields
where mice and spiders hide
under rocks, where deer shelter,
their mouths soft and rounded
as though they could speak
only to children.

Symbols

4 *Digital*

>Password: deadmantalking,
>a memory box of usernames, contacts,
>phone numbers, photographs, keys
>to online banking, messages
>from anyone and everyone @crazy.

>Frequent prompts left unanswered,
>the dead man's handle
>on a speeding train,
>'Regret to inform' messages
>to named recipients,

>Facebook set to 'Friends only',
>final status update: #hero.

Symbols

Musical

Desert Island Discs

1. *Fanfare for the Common Man* by Aaron Copeland
2. *Sharpe's Love Farewell* (Traditional, arr. Purvey)
3. *High on the Hill*, Alan Moorhouse, 1970s trumpet solo
4. *Over the Hills and Far Away*, 17th century folksong, with solo piccolo to close
5. *Light Division Assembly* bugle flourish
6. *The Road to the Isles* Regimental double-past
7. *I Vow to Thee My Country* by Sir Cecil Spring-Rice and Gustav Holst
8. *The Last Post*

Book: SAS Training Manual.
Luxury: A boat or a length of rope.

Symbols

6 *Ritualistic*

Tomo kept a ticket
for the Arctic Monkeys at the O2
from their last date

in his pocket, like a lucky
scratch-card, his front door key
on a chain round his neck –

the *Don't wait up* message
to his mum, as though
she wouldn't listen

for the strangers at the door,
one light left on, fooling no one.

Twinning

London Olympic Park, 2012

Is there anywhere on Earth
like Helmand? Least of all London,
any more than a unicorn
is like a camel

in broad terms, aside
from their flying pace, both feet
on the same side, moving together.

Now missiles on rooftops
make ready for kite fights
in the East, speed bumps
ripped up for visitors

from friend-cities, sworn-brother
provinces, flags diving
and tumbling like pigeons. Here,

snipers like tigers, shapeless
in the long grass, guard ancient woodlands
filled with water dropworts

fresh as antelope. There, a tank commander
scans the sky for pelicans, tracks

         the zigzag surge

of goitered gazelles, snow leopards
sculpted from winter memory.

On Pen Y Fan

(for reservists LCpl Craig Roberts, Trooper Edward Maher and Cpl James Dunsby who died following a 16-mile SAS Selection march on Pen Y Fan in 13th July 2013)

> We are not fit to lead an army unless we are familiar with the face of the country...
>
> SUN TZU, *The Art of War*, *c.* 550 BC

My father trained commandos
here. He knew her face, though
he only saw one eye, one nostril
at a time, her ear turned always
to the night-faring sea.

But her lips could carry a tune,
high as buzzards
with Hallelujah hands
and you must dance.

He never walked
without marching, never marched
without whistling, pitched his boys
off hilltops in great hooped staves –
'Roll out the Barrel', 'Kiss me goodnight,

Sergeant-Major, be a mother to me,'
watched each bird-boned shepherd scud
across the skyline, swinging
his rescued lamb like a dropped stitch.

He taught them how to follow flies
and finches straight and low
to water, to clean their teeth with ash,
make sleeping shadows feathered

with shirts and borrowed clouds,
how to bribe a cow with sweating palms, read
good weather backwards, right to left,
the wind behind.

He would have told you
how the thirsty sun wraps
you in her spider silk and drinks,
pours you into shadows
shredded between rocks
and turns your spit to soot.

Binary

Bulford, Wiltshire, 14th November 2013

> The aim of a joke is not to degrade the human being but to
> remind him that he is already degraded.
>
> George Orwell

The computer doesn't know fact
from fiction, isn't programmed
for Yossarian paradoxes or throttled

by loops of closed logic.

No one wins

or loses, its binary star drawing
our laughter with its own gravity. Yet
it knows the preferred word-count

for the world's funniest joke is
one-hundred-and-three, a happy prime,
though in Ukraine, India, Belarus

it brings the medics running...

This year's joke: two hunters
from New Jersey, a fallen man, his eyes rolled back,
a voice on the telephone, calm and soothing,

Take it easy. First, let's make sure he's dead.
Silence. Then a shot is heard. The hunter's voice,
OK, now what?

The computer doesn't care if the hunters
are hunters, if the fallen man has grenades,
an AK47, that the actual words were,

It's nothing you wouldn't
have done to us... Now shuffle off this mortal coil...
time, for him, already unwinding.

One-hundred-and-three,

thirty-nine degrees, give or take, already
a fever, not unexpected there,
at that time of year.

Blast Wave

You don't hear it. First, the thump
in your chest, fistfuls of memories
with poisoned fingernails. Nothing moves

except your eyeballs, bouncing,
slamming into walls, cheap furniture, dangerous
corners where the wave is strongest. You say,

There was a boy,

man-trapped in the broken frame
of his compound, his child years
shaken, severed like kite string,

the debt his father pays
for a missing goat. His screams
spike and fall, rattle in your helmet,

There was a boy

plucks your spine senseless. He must dance
and you must listen
as they take their turn with him,

scalp-locks of his hair between
their fingers, milk teeth souvenirs
for each trophy necklace.

Battle Shock

They say that poppies love nothing
more than battlefields, playing dead
for fifty years, nuzzling
unclaimed bones, cold as moons –
an arm, a leg below the knee, boot
still attached, singed fragments
of someone sinking in a ditch, sweeping
his arms like a shrimp. They say,
when the soil's disturbed, sixty thousand
seeds burst out, faster than bullets, a city
of flowers.

For now, you close curtains, turn
off lights, make strange friendships
with words you've never used before, pace
your room at midnight, can't rest
unless your back and chest
are touching something.

At the sun's slow digging, you wake shouting
for your boots, while I light fires,
burn logs that glow
like elephant dung, watch fences, keep
always a whip and chair between us,
place flowers at every blown-out window.

Ringside Mama

> Ah, but a man's reach should exceed his grasp,
> Or what's a heaven for?

ROBERT BROWNING

No one could take a punch
like Ali: *left, right, left, right,*
beached on the ropes,
sliding his neck down his spine
like a turtle, only eyes

and nostrils showing above the horny
ridges of his gum shield. Too tired
to make a song and dance with his cudgel
verse, *Float like a butterfly,*

*sting like a bee. His hands can't hit
what his eyes can't see.* Rapid-fire, *left,
right, left, right:* jab, uppercut,
hook, right hand coming in behind,

the stinging head-shots
seen too late. *Left, right, left, right,*
punch and dodge, every limb
moving, like a galloping horse,
the low guard, the swan-neck clinch.

Left... right... left... right,
your slow march, the Ali shuffle,
tipping from toe to heel, freezing
in doorways, saved by the bell

as the telephone rings, too far away
to answer. *This is the legend
of Muhammad Ali, the greatest
fighter that ever will be.*

Left… right, eighty inches,
across his chest, finger
reaching for the finger
that now can't find his nose,

feet floating in mid-air,
days of the week written
on his knuckles.

Left… right… left… right… left… right.

Child-proofing

All of humanity's problems stem from man's inability to sit
quietly in a room alone...

BLAISE PASCAL

Once again we're on our knees
to see how things look
from there. This is no place

for glass, china, anything
heavier than a bird's egg. No room
for dens of blankets over chairs, sheets

thin enough for ghosts
to hide behind, as we blunt
the corners of unspoken things,

lock away knives, tablets, paper-clips,
fit window locks, test the length
and stretch of curtain cords, knowing

how the weight of your own head
can overbalance you, like a TV
tipped over, news falling

on you as we push you
out of reach.

Repatriation

Remembering 18th August 2011

On Wootton Bassett High Street, Monet paints
straight to canvas, no retouching, his parasol
and easel pitched between the British Legion bikers

and outliers with nothing
to do, the shops being shut, his palette
every colour except black

or white because life's not like that, if
it ever was, especially for them. He paints
the biker's red bandana bright

as wet pebbles, lilies cobalt-blue, traffic lights
the changing colours of the sun, makes ribs
of timbered houses rise

again and, in the foreground, hides
the loved and lost in shadows so deep
and full of colour, they struggle to stand.

BRYONY DORAN

BULLETPROOF

(2016)

BULLETPROOF

The poems in Bryony Doran's *Bulletproof* tell a chronological story, from her son's unexpected decision to join the army through his tour in and return from Afghanistan. Covering every emotion from fear to fury, yet lifted by humour and details of everyday domestic life, these are poems written to preserve a pacifist mother's sanity as each day plays itself out. They show her coping with the daily news, her fantasies, his short spell of home leave, and her realisation that both are imprisoned in a modern myth.

Bryony Doran's first novel, *The China Bird*, won the Hookline novel competition in 2008 and was published in 2009, and followed in 2013 by her short story collection, *The Sand Eggs*. She has written and performed poetry for many years and completed an MA in Writing at Sheffield Hallam University. Her first collection, *Bullet Proof*, is first published here in *Home Front*. Born in a youth hostel on Dartmoor, she grew up in Cornwall and studied fashion at Manchester before moving to Yorkshire. She lives in Sheffield with her partner Bill Allerton, who is also a writer, and has one son.

http://www.bryonydoran.com

FOREWORD

I first met Bryony Doran while teaching a workshop in Crete and was knocked sideways by the voice, as well as subject matter, of her poems. I had read powerful poetry testimonies of war written by soldiers themselves; Bryony's poems revealed the mother's side of things. She was a prose fiction writer but to address this crucial experience she had turned to poetry and I worked with her a while to help her shape, select, and let the poems tell their archetypal story in their grainily individual detail.

However difficult it is for a mother to see her son go off to combat, when writing poems it is all too easy to overdo emotion. Real heartbreak can come across as stagey and embarrassing. Bryony gives us all the emotion but distances it, and sets it in shifting perspectives, through her unquenchable irony, dry humour, her gift for the implicit and her hair-trigger sensitivity to unexpected details, including the language in which the army communicates to parents.

The poems follow a chronological arc from her son's unexpected announcement that he has joined up to his tour of duty, return to Afghanistan, and coming home, whole and safe, for good. They cover every emotion, from terror through nostalgia to fury, with superbly controlled laconic economy. In her effort to make sense of what is happening, she varies the ways she looks at herself: sometimes she is 'I', sometimes a 'you' or a 'she'. Brought up a pacifist, she has to come to terms with her son's decision. Her father went to jail for his pacifist principles, 'Hand-sewing mail-bags with a missing index finger, / never meeting his daily quota, getting his rations cut'. What would he say to his grandson going off from Brize Norton to Afghanistan? What is happening to her child – a body she brought into the world and used to keep safe, a mind she has seen develop but now suddenly the mind of a soldier – and to her, his mother?

The desire to look after him flickers through a series of parcel poems with a wry smile at the tone of the instructions. 'Advice on a Parcel for Theatre', 'Afghanistan Must Not Appear in the Address', 'Sending a Parcel to *Your* Soldier'. She too is now part of the army, 'another dazed parent' told what to look out for on his home leave.

'PTSD symptoms can take decades to appear'; 'More soldiers have committed suicide than have died in Afghanistan' ('Tips for Parents of Returning Soldiers'). Even before he goes, she gets a taste of what's to come through tactless things people say. 'He'll never get a proper night's sleep again. / I suppose I shouldn't have told you that should I?'

She gets a new app, so she can have on her iPhone the time of day in Kabul as well as Britain. 'I can see when I am having breakfast / he'll be eating lunch.' The shifts of perspective keep everything vivid. In her fantasies of what life is like out there, she imagines 'a small boy / climbing a tree in a walled orchard' to bring in the pomegranate harvest, and then the soldiers as that boy sees them. Even she cannot recognise her son among them ('In their desert fatigues they all look the same') but she knows that all the soldiers will be suspicious of the boys in the trees and of 'the soft grenades/that land with a thud and a rupture of flesh.'

As she copes with daily news bulletins, her own fantasies and his tense spell of home leave (return to Afghanistan hanging over them), she realises they are both part of that 'theatre' of myth. She distils the pain and powerless anger this mythic but frighteningly present scenario evokes in poems shot through with ironic self-awareness, dry quick wit, and lively details of everyday life.

Underneath everything runs the relationship with her child, and what they cannot 'tell' each other now. ('With the remote he picks the dub option./ I'd prefer subtitles but stay silent/ and settle for a language we both understand.') Finally in the last poem, when he's back, she realises that telling does not matter. They have both had the same thought and not told it. Somewhere, whatever has happened, they both feel 'the same.'

These are spare, compassionate poems written to preserve a mother's sanity, often funny but also gripping and very moving. In a dry, unflinchingly fresh and original voice, they tell a story as old as poetry itself but also horribly contemporary.

RUTH PADEL

BULLETPROOF

Joining Up

He didn't tell me, until after he'd given up his job,
that he wasn't sure he'd actually get through

or that when he went to sign for Queen and Country
I could've dressed up and gone along with him.

The first time I saw him in uniform he didn't tell me
he'd be a stranger who swore like a trooper in front of his mother

or that I'd become part of the army, another dazed parent
eating plastic packed sandwiches thrown casually on tables.

He didn't tell me that in order to pass muster, he'd make up his bed
then without even a blanket sleep all night on the floor

or that when it got to November, as part of his training,
he'd spend a week in the snow on the North Yorkshire moors.

At Passing Out, he didn't tell me that with rifles as props, they'd strut
debonair as horses, then swoop forward and stoop to a bow

or that in the Officer's Mess tonic wasn't served without gin
and I'd meet his sergeant, a man they called Sheepteeth

who said my son was known for his droll humour
an opportune comment that always raised the morale.

He didn't tell me that after we left, he'd get paralytic, miss the last
          train
and then get a taxi to bring him the hundred miles home.

Hey Joe

It wafts in from my own teenage years,
and now from the gap under the attic door,
on his first day off in six weeks,

he plays it over and over.
'I said, where you goin with that gun in your hand?'
After four decades, I now understand. These recruits

in barracks, who still survive,
who hang on in there –
every last one of them is Joe.

Things People Say

Did you know
it'll send him mental?
He'll have to block everything out,
never get a proper night's sleep again

and when he Passes Out did you know
they have to jump out of aeroplanes
over Iceland or Canada, somewhere cold anyway,
without even a proper parachute

and if they land on a lake and go through the ice
they die but if they don't they have to lie there
spread eagled for forty-eight hours
waiting to be collected.

He'll never get a proper night's sleep again.
I suppose I shouldn't have told you that should I?

A Pre-tour Talk

I'm in a hall of strangers
listening to a man in uniform,
except his mic's not working
and we're only getting half the words.
The lads are outside fagging it.

I'm terrible with it, terrible.
A mother next to me says
I've stopped telling people
They say he'll be fine.
How do they know?

Her name's Julie, we exchange emails
and later share fears we can't voice.
Now there's a woman on stage with crutches.
She tells us she's a 7/7 survivor,
grateful to our lads for protecting our country.

Advice on a Parcel for Theatre

From chatting to those in theatre
we understand that everything is welcome.
It really is the thought that counts!
The key is to include small things
as the accumulative weight soon adds up.

Travel sizes are ideal rather than a family pack.
Variety is important too – it's much nicer to receive a box
filled with lots of different things rather than say, toiletry items.
Remember these are morale-boosting parcels –
The lads and lassies are being well fed and watered!

Words taken from *A guide for the families of deployed regular Army Personnel.*

AWOL

What if he were to bottle it, go AWOL
on this last weekend home before Afghanistan?

Would they hunt him down like an escaped convict,
take him to the Glasshouse, lock him in the dark

and when he'd served his sentence, let him
walk away with a dishonourable discharge,

two legs and the rest of his life?

Certificate 18

I want to spend time with him before he goes
and suggest we watch a film together.

He selects *The Girl with the Dragon Tattoo*
thinking I'll object but I don't.

With the remote he picks the dub option.
I'd prefer subtitles but stay silent

and settle for a language we both understand.
He turns out the lights.

Macaroni Cheese

For his last meal he asks for a simple dish,
one you always made when he was ill as a child.
You clatter pasta into a pan of hot water
and add a dollop of oil to stop the bonding.
You don't cheat, as you normally would, but make a roux,
let the butter melt to gold before adding the flour
and then with a wooden spoon, stir to Play-Doh.
Now for the difficult part, as you stir adding cold milk,
praying the lumps will all dissolve, admiring the motion
of your wrist as the sauce begins to thicken and you can
add the cheese he grated earlier. Oh mustard!
You find the tin at the back of the cupboard, prise off
the metal lid and scoop out yellow powder paint.
When the pasta is cooked, you add it to the sauce
then pour into the old Pyrex dish you always use.
For decoration a sprinkle of cheese and a dusting
of paprika. Or cayenne? You never can remember.
You could shout up the stairs and ask, or
riffle through the pages of *Good Housekeeping*
and wonder how you'll be tomorrow,
the start of your sentence from October
through to (you count off on your fingers) May.
You'll block it out in your diary, tick off each day,
each night, each week he's still alive.
An ice cream van drives up the side street.
You wait for 'Lara's Theme'. Today, it's a soldier song:
Yankee doodle went to town riding on a pony
Put a feather is his cap and called it macaroni.
You sit down with a cup of tea. He joins you,
takes his first mouthful, asks if there's seconds.

In the Event Of

Check, he's written a will.
Says he has

that he's taken out life insurance.
I tell him he shouldn't have bothered.

Is there a sealed envelope in the event of?
Says he doesn't bother with such things.

Wormwood Scrubs

Seeing you stood to attention I see my father
and wonder what he'd say if he were alive,

waving his only grandchild off to war,
his pacifist principles thrown in his face.

Hand-sewing mail-bags with a missing index finger,
never meeting his daily quota, getting his rations cut,

if he'd known then that you'd choose to become a soldier,
would he have banged on his cell door and shouted

to be let out, seeing that all his struggles were for nothing,
or would he have kept shtum and done his term?

I wonder, would he blame me for bringing you up wrong
or shake you by the hand – *look after yerself me old cock.*

Flight to Kandahar

Tonight thirty-three Chilean miners
trapped underground for sixty-nine days
rise one by one through the earth in a capsule
their arms tucked back like cormorants gliding upwards
until they come finally into the light
to their families and the rest of the world.

At Brize Norton two thousand men in desert fatigues
rise into the night sky plane after plane
a formation of large grey birds migrating south
for Addis Ababa to refuel then on to Kandahar
and finally Nar-e-Saraj, to remain
for one-hundred-and-seventy-two days.

In the Shower

I list the benefits of his going
they play over and over in my head
however I try to silence them.

No piss on the toilet mat.
No nights of him lurching in drunk.
No mounds of dirty washing.

My writing-room back.
Never knowing whether to cook or not,
him turning up unannounced on a Friday night.

His going back to camp, always a dash,
a mad drive to catch the last train.
That blank feeling on a Sunday night.

The pull of the cord, a click, his obsession
to always turn the shower off at the mains
however many times I tell him.

Now, when I go for a pee in the night
my shower is on standby,
an orange lozenge glowing in the dark.

The Cleansing

1974

I'm a fashion student at Manchester. I get ill
and my flatmate, who's studying Russian literature,
kindly offers to lend me *And Quiet Flows the Don.*

– A Cossack son goes to fight on the Turkish front.
His mother sorts away an unwashed shirt,
and when she misses him she breathes his sweat –

I put the book aside until I'm feeling stronger
then pick it up where I left off and read on to the end,
and ask to borrow *The Don Flows Home to the Sea.*

2010

He always wears white cotton t-shirts,
spills Coca-Cola and pizza down the front,
knowing his mother can get anything out.

When he goes to fight in Afghanistan
I sort his whites, darks, and delicates.
Open the yellowed pages of my book.

And Quiet Flows the Don and *The Don Flows Home to the Sea* by Mikhail
Sholokhov, winner of the Nobel Prize in Literature in 1965.

Waiting Days

I have just visited Plath's grave with my friend Liz.
We're in a café having tea. A youth wearing a cycle hat
comes through the door letting in the cold.
His cheeks are slap red and when he takes off
his hat he has flaxen hair that suits his complexion,
unlike my son, with his black, black hair.
It's three weeks since he flew out.
Still no word.

Driving back over Emley Moor I wonder if he's phoned.
I want to go home but am persuaded into a curry.
After we've eaten we're so busy talking, the waiter
has to ask me to pass my plate. I think of my son.
If he were here, remembering his waiting days,
he would've stacked the plates, placed the cutlery on top,
nodded when the waiter thanked him,
's'alright mate'.

Afghanistan Must Not Appear in the Address

To use the free MOD Postal Packet Scheme
parcels are limited to 2 kilos in weight
and Royal Mail box size 2 or a small shoe box.
(Multiple parcels can be sent at any one time.)
Complete a customs sticker
itemising the contents of your parcel.
Goods that should not be sent
are: Aerosols – hairspray, deodorant.
Perishables – foods like fruit, meat and cheese.
Fragile items – glass etc. And magazines
containing pictures that might offend
the cultural values of a host nation.
'Top Shelf' are an obvious example.
Alcohol and lighters are strictly prohibited
Packets may only be sent to named personnel
using number, name, rank and BFPO number.
Your parcel must be taken to a post office
not put straight into a post box.
Afghanistan must not appear in the address.

Words taken from *A guide for the families of deployed regular Army Personnel.*

First Call Home

'Alright Mum.
Sorry I haven't phoned before

tried yesterday but there was a queue
then something kicked off and operations shut down.

I haven't woke you have I?
Oh God I'm sorry I forgot, the clocks go back.

Its okay here, better than Catterick,
we do stuff

not that we've done much yet
just been out on patrol

and we're building a silo
and handing out grain

hearts and minds ya know
its weird, s'like stepping back centuries.

Where are we? At a checkpoint
near Camp Bastion, 'bout ten minutes by chopper.

We're in a big tent, ten of us, with mosquito nets.
Fucking cold at night.

Some parcels 'ud be good, DVDs, some mags,
don't take any notice of their advice

and some sweets and pens for the kids round here.
Little shits keep chucking stones.

Well I'd better go, me mate wants the phone.
See ya Mum.'

Snow on the Line

I have a compulsion to tell strangers on trains,
My son is in Afghanistan.
A man, who sits next to me, on the way back
from Newcastle, asks how do I cope?
Swirling snow blurs the landscape.
I don't know where we are.
At Durham I move seats to face the right way
but when I go to the toilet a youth moves my coat
and takes my seat. He's plugged in to a war film.
I know he's a soldier, I can read the signs.
Outside Darlington we stop for snow on the line.
I say, *'You're a soldier.' 'A Marine,'* he corrects.
Then I say it, *'My son's in Afghanistan.'*
He looks at me, no pity in his eyes.
He's been. It's tough. Can't wait to go back.
At York I move seats, I want to face the wrong way,
read all the Sunday papers held at arms length:
3 soldiers injured in a roadside bomb in Helmand.
The trains stops, we're outside Doncaster.
Snow on the line.

The World Clock

On my iPhone I have a new app
that shows night dark-faced and day pale
in both London and Kabul.
I can see when I am having breakfast
he'll be eating lunch.
On the *Today Programme* at 6.02 a.m.
They report the death of a soldier.
The first, since he left.

Sending a Parcel to *Your* Soldier

I cast my mind back to when he was child,
Smarties, Galaxy, A Finger of Fudge,
Rowntrees Wine Gums, Jelly Babies, oh
and Liquorice Allsorts.
Parkin, he always had a liking for parkin,
and Marmite, lots of it on buttered toast.
I peruse the supermarket shelves for ideas:
Extra Mature Cheddar, Jacob's Cream Crackers,
sachets of hot chocolate, Ribena, peanut butter
– and jam sandwiches, his favourite packed lunch.
What flavour crisps was he partial to?
I could bake a cake, he'd like that.
Now what was it he wanted from the chemist?
Toothpaste, foot powder, zinc plasters, deodorant.
(Things you'd think the army would provide.)
He doesn't want soap, they've no water.
Mouthwash – diluted with vodka!
At the newsagents, I buy two top shelf magazines
then go back home and sort through the DVDs
Dave down the pub gave me: *Edge of Darkness,*
The Men Who Stare at Goats, Death at a Funeral.
'All free for our lads out there.'
I prepare for my weekly trip to the Post Office.
Scour the kitchen cupboards for the scales.
Fill the shoeboxes to 1.98 kilograms.
I do not unseal the mouthwash, but put in some JD toffees
then secure the box twice with gaffer tape.
Maybe next week I'll have the energy to bake a cake.
I write on his address, number and BFPO location,
put anything that comes to mind on the customs form.
At the post office I bring to the attention
of the postmaster that it's a free MOD package.
When he demands payment because it's too heavy
I do not lose my temper but march back up the hill,
slit the tape and take out the salt and vinegar crisps
then return to the post office.

The Junior Officers' Reading Club

I pick it up from Waterstones,
the third in a three-for-two book offer,
to put in a morale-boosting parcel,
but before I send it, I dip and dip again,
then wrap it with the cheese and chocolate
and return to Waterstones to buy my own copy.

I cheat time and finds gaps in the day.
The testosterone of combat
seeps into my brain, my blood.
For the first time I get it –
this is a path he's chosen.
I'll write to Mr Hennessey and thank him.

The Junior Officers' Reading Club by Patrick Hennessey.

A Break in the Fighting

Friends ask me the date of his R&R,
tell me I must be looking forward to it,
I smile, remain silent.

They keep moving his dates
nearer to when he'd come home for good.
What's the point, he'd be better not coming.

They could send him to some Middle East resort.
That would be a holiday for all of us,
knowing he was safe, getting some beer and sun.

Floods in Queensland

The dark is a dry well where sleep evades me
until I fall to dream out on patrol with you

on a cold moon night walking in single file,
afraid of pressing earth, of twigs breaking.

An explosion. A blast of furnace heat.
I'm ripped from sleep. The radio alarm

tells of catastrophic floods in Queensland.
But no hint of an incident in Nar-e-Saraj.

The Winter Hares

When you come home on leave,
will you seek out alone
a place with big sky
and mountains where the harrier soars,
will you walk until you can walk no further,
from day into night,
then hitch a ride home in the pitch black
like that time those bastards sacked you so unfairly –
or will you walk with me
on Derwent Edge
see the white hares in February
and remember the stoats we searched for,
every school holiday,
for years?

Rest & Relaxation

He steps off the train in his desert fatigues,
the only clothes he's got with him.
Old men on the journey home have wanted
to shake him by the hand, *good on yer lad*.
At first he goes out with friends, gets drunk
but he is sick to death of being asked
the same questions so he stays in.
He's not hungry, doesn't want me to cook,
orders pizza online I know nothing about
until there's a knock on our back door.

A face on the TV, a soldier killed in Afghanistan,
a lad he shared a room with during training:
Fucking loved the army, wanted to be SAS.
I hear him late at night pacing his attic room,
then opening the cupboard door to get his shoes,
taking himself off for a walk and a smoke.
On his last day he says when he gets back
he's putting in for his motorbike test.
He sees the look on my face and laughs,
asks why I'm scared of life.

Bulletproof

On our landing there's a bulletproof vest
I keep stubbing my toe on.
It doesn't budge, unlike his helmet
that rolls like a decapitated head.

Had to wear them as we were flying
out of Kandahar
in case we got shot down
– daft I know.

The fatigues he brought back
were full of desert grit that dried my finger ends,
now they hang drying over the banister,
the sleeves still rolled up.

His army issue underpants
spill tiny white beads over the landing carpet.
They're special, he says.
Saves yer manhood if you get yer legs blown off.

Return to Afghanistan

In the control room I'm asked for my car registration
and when I laugh and say I don't know it, my son
marches off to find out in the four o'clock dark
whilst I watch a grey screen looking for planes

destined for Kandahar from here at Brize Norton
but all I can see is one due in from Minneapolis.
When we've been cleared, I drive across base,
we don't speak. I look for Departures.

I open the boot, and with a sling of his Bergen
onto his shoulder – a quick hug, *see you mum*,
(You don't have to go back – unspoken) he's gone.
Through the window I see him jostling his mates.

Back at the hotel room I find our unmade beds
we slept in for an hour, the door jamb he lent against,
dressed in full combat. The photo I took.
Scrolling my phone I see the boy behind a man.

Thesaurus

See – that word is there again.
When I look for *motherhood*

the page falls once more to *hinterland* –
uncharted territories of scrub – a no-man's-land.

That's where I thought we were.
You out there, beckoning.

The Dressing Gown

She is delaying the morning ritual:
showering, cleaning her teeth, getting dressed,
the unkindness of every day repeating itself,

tasks folding from yesterday into today:
cleaning the toilet, the kitchen floor, hand-washing.
Jobs that require rubber gloves

and onions, the chopping and frying of onions.
She'll get washed soon, start a new day
with her hair smelling of apple and chamomile.

The postman knocks, brings a package
from a world where other people live.
What if they were to come to the back door

with her in her dressing gown smelling of onions?
She'd have to send them to stand on the pavement,
take a quick shower, dress and do her teeth.

They'd hold their berets by the rim, look down
at their shoes. She'd hear their words in her kitchen.
– Could they make her a cup of sweet tea?

Preparation for Theatre

It must be six years, almost to the day.
You were seventeen, still at home,
not out in a war zone as you are now.

You had an appointment with the dental surgeon
(Mr Smith, a man I trusted instantly.)
He picked up a skull, held it in his spread hand,

showed us where he would break your jaw
upper and lower, in two places.
How he would slit the roof of your mouth.

It had been years since I passed out.
He laid me in a pale green dentist's chair
and fed me water from a plastic cup.

When I felt able to sit up
I saw your face. You were angry at me.
Insisted we get the bus back up the hill.

Harvest

I hear on the radio, talk of the pomegranate harvest
in Nar-e-Saraj, and in my head I see a small boy
climbing a tree in a walled orchard

to tap the leathery rind of each fruit in turn,
and if he hears a chime like a dull bell
I see him cup the fruit either side of the calyx crown

and with a quick twist, sever it from the tree
then lob it into the long grass where his older brother
is waiting for the catch to add to his wicker basket.

I see soldiers skirting the perimeter.
One of them could be my son I can't tell,
in their desert fatigues they all look the same.

They are suspicious of the soft grenades
that land with a thud and a rupture of flesh
if the small boy is quicker than his brother.

I see how, from up in the tree the small boy
can watch the soldiers with their guns. He is not afraid,
they give him pens and play football with him

when the elders are away in the town.
I see that if the small boy took careful aim
he could hit one of the tin helmets

but these soldiers who are a similar age
to his brother do not deserve his prized fruit,
and though I see he is sorely tempted

we both know
that the response would be
an unseasonal rain of bullets.

Doing John Agard for GCSE

No dawdling that day,
you fairly loped home from school, exploding
through the front door into my work room.

I laid down my black handled shears,
and switched off the sewing machine.
You fetched the biscuits, I made a brew,

then we sat on my unmade bed and drank tea,
yours with one sugar and chocolate digestives.
You told me about a John Agard poem,

standing to give a rendition in front of my mirror.
Always the natural mimic, the class clown
you plagued us for days.

Explain yuself
Standing on one leg
wha yu mean
when yu say half-caste?

How did we get snuck up on?
You out there in Afghanistan manning a checkpoint,
a delayed voice asking for thermal socks,

me here in front of my full-length mirror,
hearing kids return from school, doing my exercises,
trying to strengthen my core, to balance on one leg,

pulling my foot up behind, to hold for thirty seconds.
And there you are in my mirror
– Standing on one leg.

The News from Your Area

The news woman has another *veteran* story.
A local man, who died in Sangeen Province
fighting for his country, is to have a Close
in Nottingham named after him.

She interrogates his parents. Wants to know.
How did it happen? How does it feel?
How can you cope? How did you hear?
A man and a woman came to our door

wearing civilian clothing. My partner
– reaches for the remote. I grab it –
the woman said she was a Major.
That's when we knew...

No. That's not right. I have the picture in my head:
two men in military uniform come to our door
announce to us, and the street, why they've come.
Not a couple we might mistake for Jehovah's Witnesses.

End of Tour

He should have been out of there ages ago
or at least safe at Camp Bastion.
I wait and wait. No news.

On the World Service I hear
Bin Laden has been found, killed
and, as they speak, buried at sea.

At daybreak a woman
from the pub messages me:
Look on your lad's Facebook
– He's in Cyprus. Drunk!

Tips for Parents of Returning Soldiers

If you notice a change in your soldier
on his return from theatre and are worried
about him, remember you can always talk
with an army doctor in confidence.
PTSD symptoms can take decades to appear
so keep this thought at the back of your mind.

Your soldier won't admit anything's wrong,
makes you promise not to contact the army,
says he doesn't want to be seen
as a shirker or even worse, weak
and anyway it wouldn't make any difference.
Keep that thought at the back of your mind.

More soldiers have committed suicide than have died in Afghanistan.
Words taken from *A guide for the families of deployed regular Army Personnel.*

Avoiding Traffic Accidents

After an operational deployment,
some soldiers may take time
to readjust to making judgments
about taking acceptable risks
in a non-operational environment,
particularly when driving.
This has seen a reported increase
in road traffic accidents
involving soldiers post deployment.
If you or your soldier need more
information on road safety matters,
contact the Army Welfare Service.
They in turn may seek guidance
from their Regional Master Driver.

More soldiers have died in motorbike accidents since coming back than have died in Afghanistan.

Words taken from *A guide for the families of deployed regular Army Personnel.*

A Dancer

When he was a child we used to play hide-and-seek
in the long corridors of my mother's house.
Often he would secrete himself away
in a cubby-hole outside the bathroom door
and when I passed, jump out. Shout, *boo!*

He'd been two weeks back from Afghanistan
when I hid there, jumped out as he passed,
saw him move swift as a dancer, a twirl, a whirl round,
a slide to the ground.
If he'd had a gun, I'd be dead.

A Parade in the Rain

Yes I know I shouldn't have done it,
that it's your life, your story,
but where am I in all this?
You didn't have to get up at 3 a.m.
and drive down the motorway, did you?
So please don't tell me what I can and can't say.
Okay, okay, maybe, I shouldn't have gone to the *Guardian*
but you didn't have to watch all those families
who'd slept in their cars overnight
get dressed in their best, even the children,
and you weren't there when we were all stood at the memorial
in the cold, waiting for something to happen,
looking at the motorbike helmet someone had placed there
and seeing the visor blood red, reflecting the poppies,
not knowing what was going on.
So don't tell me to give it a rest.
And when it finally did kick off
it wasn't you that had to dash to the parade ground
and battle your way through all those wedding-dressed people
to catch a brief glimpse as you marched round.
You didn't have to watch Charlie and his entourage
swish in with their huge umbrellas
and listen to him say how he understood
how we all must have felt with our soldiers,
out there in Afghanistan.
So don't have a go at me.
And then his camera crew obscuring our view
so we had to push down through the barriers
and stand next to a grandmother in pink,
even her parasol shielding the rain,
but you know that's the one thing I had in common
with all those people there:
we'd all come for the same reason,
to realise it was all, at last, over.
That's what we wanted, to put it down.

So no you can't have your say,
you were stood to attention in the back row,
you didn't have to see the front line,
the wheelchairs, the lad, your friend,
with the new legs below the knee
and him having to look up
as Charlie pinned on his medal,
and then to top it all,
your medals, unbeknown to us
being doled out down the lines
by god knows who,
so don't tell me, *Mother it happened. Get over it.*
A graduation, that's what we all wanted,
that's why we'd all come,
that's why we'd re arranged our holiday
to see you stepping up there,
your names called out.
Respect. That's the word I didn't find that day.
All crowded into the Naafi like sodden rats,
dazed old people, crying children
and not a cup of tea or a bun laid on.
So don't tell me.

Me in My Nightie

The butcher, an obsequious man,
by way of making conversation
asks if I am cooking for an occasion
and for some reason I tell him my son
is in the army and I am going to cook
a meal before he goes back to camp.
That's when he tells me his son-in-law
has been in the army, and in Afghanistan.

Took me daughter down to fetch him back
and you know I can honestly say
it was the most emotional experience
I've ever had in my whole life,
all those coaches sweeping in, all those kiddies,
wives, girlfriends, mothers, and us. Waiting.
I wouldn't have missed it for the world.
Christ, still brings a tear to my eye.

My son had phoned from Cyprus telling me
it wasn't worth my while driving down
I'd only see him for twenty minutes
and when I said I'd like to come anyway
he'd told me he didn't know where
they'd land. I just accepted it.
I didn't know who to ask?
I wasn't there for his homecoming.

At one o'clock the next morning
the doorbell rang and there he was
on my doorstep, a tired stranger and me
in my nightie not knowing what to feel.
A mate's parents had given him a lift back.
Their son had gone off with his girlfriend
so they'd been glad of his company,
even bought him a meal as he'd no money.

By the Way

For the most part information is conveyed in company,
usually when we're all sitting in my back room
with the Schiele urchin staring at us from the chimney breast
and as a rule they are my friends and it is evening
so often drink is involved
                              as there was on this occasion
thanks to it being a year to the day since his return
so we were celebrating and he was pouring everyone
a glass of red wine when he happened to mention
he'd got some good news, news he'd kept meaning to tell me
but always kept forgetting and actually he'd known
for three weeks; he remembered it was the day
they received their wage slips and their lance corporal
had come in and told them they'd never ever have to go back
to Afghanistan ever again
sorry mum I should've mentioned it earlier shouldn't I?

Looking Back

He said, after he came back, his biggest fear
hadn't been losing his life but his legs.
He'd have had to live with that all his life.
If he'd died that would have been that.
I didn't tell him I'd thought the same.

JEHANNE DUBROW

STATESIDE

(2010)

STATESIDE

Driven by intellectual curiosity and emotional exploration, the poems in Jehanne Dubrow's *Stateside* are remarkable for their subtlety, sensual imagery and technical control. The speaker attempts to understand her own life through the long history of military wives left to wait and wonder, invoking Penelope's plight in Homer's *Odyssey* as a model but also as a source of mystery. Dubrow is fearless in her contemplation of the far-reaching effects of war but even more so in her excavation of a marriage under duress.

Jehanne Dubrow is the author of six poetry collections, including *Dots & Dashes* (Southern Illinois University Press, 2017), *The Arranged Marriage* (University of New Mexico Press, 2015), *Red Army Red* (Northwestern, 2012) and *Stateside* (Northwestern, 2010), the latter first published in the UK here in *Home Front*. She also co-edited *The Book of Scented Things: 100 Contemporary Poems about Perfume* (Literary House Press, 2014) and *Still Life with Poem: Contemporary Natures Mortes in Verse* (Literary House Press, 2016).

The daughter of American diplomats, and wife of a serving US naval officer deployed to the Persian Gulf and other conflict zones, she was born in Italy and grew up in Yugoslavia, Zaire, Poland, Belgium, Austria, and the United States. She is an associate professor of creative writing at the University of North Texas.

http://jehannedubrow.com

FOREWORD

As I read the poems in this remarkable and moving collection, I was reminded again and again of the wool sweaters knitted by the wives of Irish fishermen. According to tradition, each sweater is made with its own unique design, a combination of knots, cables, and braids, so that if the fisherman's body should wash up along the coast, his widow can identify him.

It takes skilful hands and a good many hours to make a sweater, and the person knotting and tying the yarn must keep her eye on the task, making precise decisions as she proceeds. That's the manner in which the best poems are written, too, with consummate thought and care. And one can easily imagine what might go through a woman's mind as she works, what intimations of providence she feels as she knits beside her window opening onto the impersonal, silencing sea.

These well-crafted poems by Jehanne Dubrow are, at least for this one reader, like those beautiful and altogether necessary sweaters. They have been patiently, thoughtfully, and artfully knitted by a sometimes anguished, sometimes resigned, and always hopeful young woman, well acquainted with the perils of the sea, the perils of war, the perils of loneliness, seeing her husband's ship just a spot on the horizon, sailing away.

Of course, Dubrow recognises the antiquity and depth of tradition of which these poems are a part and a continuance. Women have suffered these fearful absences for countless centuries. Those poems in which she identifies with Penelope attest to that. And the poet's responses to uncertainty are as various as are those of the generations of women who have waited, stateside, for their men to return.

In Ezra Pound's translation of a thousand-year-old Old English poem, 'The Seafarer', an anonymous sailor says,

> May I, for my own self, song's truth reckon,
> Journey's jargon, how I in harsh days
> Hardship endured oft.

Well, that's the sailor's side of it, isn't it? You are about to read the other side of the hardship, in the carefully cast words of the wife left on shore.

TED KOOSER

STATESIDE

Part One

Secure for Sea

maritime terminology

It means the moveable stays tied.
Lockers hold shut. The waves don't slide
a metal box across the decks,
or scatter screws like jacks, the sea
a rebellious child that wrecks
all tools which aren't fastened tightly
or fixed.
       At home, we say *secure*
when what we mean is letting go
of him. And even if we're sure
he's coming back, it's hard to know:
the farther out the vessel drifts,
will contents stay in place, or shift?

Assateague Island, March

We toss our coffee on the sand, watching
the liquid sink and fade to almost nothing
like disappearing ink. The wind disturbs
our tent flap, jostles the poles, sways the frame
so that I hope we cannot stay the night.
Why don't we leave? I ask. He shakes his head,
and in my borrowed sleeping bag I lie
awake, shiver beneath its summer weight,
curl myself into a question mark.
I listen, for hours, to the pace of waves
an irritant like sand inside a shoe.
He always shuts his eyes before I do.
He's slumped in front of the TV or pinned
by an opened book across his chest, and here
surrounded by the racket nature makes,
he rests, so deep asleep I don't exist.
At 8 a.m., we stand, roll up our beds.
I couldn't sleep at all, he says. *Too cold,
though you seemed fine*. I laugh. To think
of all those hours I listened for his breath
and he for mine, the air a frozen wing,
the wild ponies snuffling for food.
Goddamn our domesticity. At least
we should have sighed the other's name, or rubbed
together, tried burning like two broken sticks.

O' Dark Hundred

This is the hour that writers eulogise,
       midnights when my husband guards his post
against monotony. Before sunrise,
       this is the hour that writers eulogise.
In port, a sentry walks the deck, replies
       all conditions normal, surveys the coast.
This is the hour that writers eulogise,
       midnights when my husband guards his post.

I can imagine that he faces west,
       the sky like a purple sail above the sea.
Somewhere a buoy creeks. Waves sink or crest,
       and I imagine him. He faces west
to stand and watch and wait alone, the rest
       of the crew asleep in the machinery.
I can imagine him. He's facing west,
       the sky a purple sail above the sea.

My words are just reflections from the shore,
       and the page, imperfect mirror of his ship,
where white lights blink above each metal door.
       My words are just reflections. On the shore
there's radio silence – no talk of war,
       only the sound of nothing, only the blip
of words reflecting distantly from shore,
       and the page, imperfect mirror of his ship.

After Visiting the USS *Anzio*

We walked the pier to see the cruiser, moored
with Kevlar lines thick as limbs, then came aboard,
where decks vibrated underneath the weight
of polished brass and perforated steel.

My husband pointed out the fire main
and cable run, explained scuttles and where
the ladders led. I don't remember much
he said, but only know he placed my hand

against a hatch to feel the engines tense,
the systems like a pulse inside my palm.
And then, the CIC, where it was calm
and quiet to the passageway –

               In war
he'll stand before the green displays of light,
evaluate a signal's frequency.
He'll chart trajectories and blips across

a screen. And all the ship will swallow him:
its hull, an ashy paint they call *haze gray*
(*haze gray and under way*, say the sailors,
kissing their wives goodbye), a silver gray

of knives, of mist which settles on the water,
a gray so like the moon, its surface strewn
with oceans, bays, and seas that tremble with
the burden of their wide tranquility.

Virginia Beach

Tonight we're kids again, all summers boring
as peacetime, our grown-up lives distant

like the barrel organ grinding through a song,
the revolution of the Ferris wheel.

If we look far enough beyond the strand,
we'll see your cruiser there, a blurred knife

that separates the water from its skin,
quiet as modern warfare often is.

Rocky road drips chocolate on your hands.
You lick each fingertip, gesture at a ship

so that it disappears behind your palm,
the naval station still within your reach,

so near we smell the breath of diesel fuel.
I would like to call it death, this thing that sticks

like marshmallows inside my mouth, gritty
with a thousand sharp particulates of sea.

Newport

You lead the puppy past the moored boat.
He nuzzles sand, runs to where the waves break,
    snaps at lacquered fish that swim near shore.
You let him off the leash, because you like
    to see the freedom of a loosened thing,
a ball releasing from a hand, a voice
    untying from the collar of the throat.
Each day you walk a little farther, then bring
    him home to me, his tail a muddy spike,
his body soggy as a kitchen mop.
    We don't wring him dry but watch him shake
the ocean out, watch him rub his face across
    the carpet until he falls asleep, sopping,
curled tightly as a seashell on the floor.

Silver Spring

Montgomery County, Md.

It's light above. Below,
inside the red-line metro,

the evening never sheds itself for day,
but curves into a passageway,

a universe of fang and tail.
We're lit by bulbs whose pale

fluorescent eyes shine on, unblinkingly.
The third rail sibilates with electricity.

And we – alone
– stand frozen by a sound, the drone

of trains, sidewinders sliding through
blue corridors, steel sinew

stretched to breaking,
metallic snakes,

their scales aluminum
instead of skin.

Warm-blooded creatures don't belong
so deeply underground. We aren't strong

enough to fight the rattlesnake,
the way it coils into wire, then slowly shakes

its body as it strikes.
We wait. The subway hisses like

a diamondback.
A shadow-monster slithers down the track.

Love in the Time of Coalition

He whispers *weapons of mass destruction*
against the sand dune of her skin. She's toxin.

She's liquid sarin. She's pure plutonium.
Her tracers burn and dim and burn again.

As last resort, he holds a congressional inquiry
about her lips. *Have you no sense of decency,*

he asks her body's gulf. She's marsh and salt,
alluvial. She's Tigris and Euphrates.

He never finds an answer for her sleep,
more sudden than shrapnel, or for her waking,

sharper than a dust storm in the desert. She's dry
instead, made empty as a wadi,

waiting for rainfall to fill her watercourse
and for the nights to carve a temporary truce.

Sea Change

Imagine this: saltwater scrubbing sand
        into my husband's skin,
his fingers pale anemones, his hands
              turned coral reef, and in
      his eyes the nacreous pearls of Ariel.
This could be my husband, drowning in the swell.

A sea change means a shift, a change of heart,
        and how the oceans turn
glass shards into a jewel, rip apart
            familiar things. Waves churn.
      The surf is a liquid body that peels
a carrier from bow to stern, the keel

bent back, steel bands pliable as kelp.
        And long before I wake,
the sailors drown. No point in calling help.
            Each night, my husband shakes
      me out of sleep. I cannot reach for him
or drag him to the surface so he'll swim.

Whiskey Tango Foxtrot

what the fuck?

Foxtrot the Navy, I yell into the phone,
the first time that my husband groans *deployed*,
a word we've waited for since war began
four years ago.
                    [Let *whiskey* slide as slow
as bullets down my throat. Let *foxtrot* be
both verb and noun.]
                                Foxtrot the Navy,
I say again but softer than before,
as if the whisper of a dance could keep
him here.
                    [I need a shot of *whiskey* just
to take the news, a song in 2/4 time
and rhinestone shoes.]
                                Foxtrot, I sigh –
third time's the charm in everything but war,
oh ugly, big sublime. I'm buzzing with
white noise.
                    [Call in the dancing girls,
the boys who swallow slugs from jerricans,
moonshine sloshed to the brim of each canteen.
Let *whiskey* taste toxic as benzene.]

Nonessential Equipment

The dog and I are first among those things
that will not be deployed with him. Forget
civilian clothes as well. He shouldn't bring
too many photographs, which might get wet,
the faces blurred. He only needs a set
of uniforms. Even his wedding ring
gives pause (what if it fell? – he'd be upset
to dent or scratch away the gold engraving).
The seabag must be light enough to sling
across his shoulder, weigh almost nothing,
each canvas pocket emptied of regret.
The trick is packing less. No wife, no pet,
no perfumed letters dabbed with *I-love-yous*,
or anything he can't afford to lose.

Swim Test

In the swimming pool, my husband is a stone
that cannot float – he's made for running
through our neighborhood, which leads him down

to where the concrete goes to gravel, then turns
to harrowed fields at the edge of town,
where wind pushes through the corn,

and the crow that drags itself up sounds like a man
drowning. All things sound like drowning if you listen.
There are other men who sink, the ones grown

up in cinderblock cities who have never seen
the beach, or the ones like my husband, too thin
for buoyancy. They have learned to inflate their own

shirts, blow bubbles of air in the sleeves, fasten
the limbs together, a raft that holds them on
the surface long enough. After a deepwater jump, then

a fifty-yard swim, the sailors lie prone.
They're flotsam drifting in the ocean.
The hardest part is playing dead, to be broken,

inert, when what the body wants is motion,
to kick like a sprinter toward the finish line,
at least to tread water, not to breathe it in.

A Short Study of Catastrophe

We're arguing about his death again.
Because all men are fools, he swears

I won't be anywhere near the fighting.
I try to laugh but can't, imagining

the photographs of Humvees overturned
like dead roaches, so burned their shells curl back

to show the viscosity inside. *Guys die
just driving from the base. The fucking place*

is cursed, I say. It's hard remaining calm.
Each conversation holds a roadside bomb,

a sniper in the window, insurgents on
the ground below. Tell me. How did the Greeks

learn beauty from that sudden turn we call
catastrophe? – the king disposed with three

quick blows, the wailing child, the wife,
and always then the falling   falling knife.

Against War Movies

I see my husband shooting in *Platoon*,
and there he is again in *M*A*S*H* (how weird
to hear him talk like Hawkeye Pierce), and soon
I spot him everywhere, his body smeared
with mud, his face bloodied. He's now the star
of every ship blockade and battle scene –
The Fighting 69th, *A Bridge Too Far*,
Three Kings, *Das Boot*, and *Stalag 17*.
In *Stalingrad* he's killed, and then
he's killed in *Midway* and *A Few Good Men*.
He's burned or gassed, he's shot between the eyes,
or shoots himself when he comes home again.
Each movie is a training exercise,
a scenario for how my husband dies.

Before the Deployment

He kisses me before he goes. While I,
still dozing, half-asleep, laugh and rub my face

against the sueded surface of the sheets,
thinking it's him I touch, his skin beneath

my hands, my body curving in to meet
his body there. I never hear him leave.

But I believe he shuts the bedroom door,
as though unsure if he should change his mind,

pull of his boots, crawl beneath the blankets
left behind, his hand a heat against my breast,

our heart rates slowing into rest. Perhaps
all goodbyes should whisper like a piece of silk –

and then the quick surprise of waking, alone
except for the citrus ghost of his cologne.

Reading Stephen Crane's 'War Is Kind' to My Husband

I packed your seabag
today: six pairs
of pants, shirts folded in
their rigid squares,

your socks balled up
like tan grenades.
I put my photo in
as well, laid

it there between
the Kevlar vest and heap
of clothes. Don't weep,
the poet warns, don't weep.

On *60 Minutes*,
a soldier turns
his face toward us, shows
the camera his burns,

small metal slivers still
embedded in
the skin, his mouth a scrap
of ragged tin.

The young man's face
was beautiful before,
smooth, unblemished as
my own. *For war*

is kind, I read. *Great is*
the battle-god
and great the auguries,
the firing squad,

the sickly green of night
vision that cuts
the darkness open at
its seams, gutted

and spilling on the sand.
Great is the Glock,
the Aegis Combat System,
the Blackhawk

circling. Great are the Ka-Bar
fighting knives,
the shells that sing through air,
as though alive.

Part Two

The Rooted Bed

One moment he seemed... Odysseus to the life –
the next, no, he was not the man she knew

The Odyssey, Book 23

I'm stateside now, my husband six-months gone.
    I think of another soldier and his wife –
they built their bedpost from an olive tree,
    roots spreading underfoot, gray branches splayed
like fingers, floorboards grassy as a lawn.
    The tree grew through the center of their life.
They slept beneath its living canopy.
    And once the wife was left alone, its shade
stroked darkened hands across her brow.
    I like to imagine that she often thought
of chopping down the trunk, fed up with boughs
    which dropped their leaves, black fruit turning to rot.
I can't help asking if, when he came home,
    did they lie together there or sleep alone?

Argos

While my husband is deployed, I name
    our puppy for the dog who recognised
        Odysseus, knew him despite disguise,
    the king dressed as a beggar but still the same

familiar scent of metal on his skin,
    that same swagger beneath the cloak of rags,
        that sinewed voice. Argos, a fleabag,
    a sack of mange, nothing but skeleton.

What kind of instinct is such loyalty?
    Bred in the bone, certain as the sound
        of waves. No wonder that the wolfhound
    barked at the beach for twenty years, the sea

remaining empty, a tarnished piece of steel.
    No wonder that he learned to sight each ship
        along the sleek horizon, yipping
    at vessels that docked, nipping the heels

of every man in Ithaca. It must
    have hurt, as though from an old wound, to wait
        those twenty years beside the palace gate.
    Each night he watched the sky fade into rust.

Like a thirst so deep it hollowed out the throat,
    like a craving for salt air – he must have known
        that it's a body's faithfulness alone
    which made him keep his vigil for the boat.

Ithaca

There's war beyond the shores. But here
    there's Dairy Queen and Taco Bell,
        the Westfield Shopping Mall, the cell
            phone superstore, Home Depot, Sears.

And home remains a metaphor
    for something else: a wife who tries
        to guard her chastity, ties
            it like a yellow ribbon to her door,

sticks it to the bumper of
    her car, so that the neighbors know
        she sleeps alone, almost a widow
            to the Trojan War, her love

preserved in plastic wrap like some
    dessert too beautiful to taste.
        At PTA meetings, she's chased
            by divorcés and other glum

suitors. Nobody seems to care
    that she still wears a wedding ring.
        Odysseus is gone – same thing
            as being dead. And so men stare

at her when she buys groceries
    or takes the dog out for a pee.
        She's Ithaca, trapped in her own body,
            an island circled by the seas.

Penelope, Stateside

On an island called America,
   start fantasising of the sex
      you had with him. Go shop for bras
        and lacy thongs at the PX,

black garters, bustier, a cream
   that leaves your body woven silk,
      a self-help book for self-esteem,
        a bag of M&Ms, skim milk

to keep you thin, and Lean Cuisine
   (you hate to cook for one). Or buy
      a pair of True Religion jeans,
        the denim pressing on each thigh

so that there's no sensation but
   blue fabric like a second skin,
      no lover's touch more intimate
        than the zipper pressing in.

But don't forget. He may come home
   so torn that purchases won't mean
      a thing, not the Posturepedic foam
        pillowtop mattress, or the sateen

duvet. He won't be satisfied –
   by eiderdowns or bedspreads sewn
      by hand – still numb, because he's stateside
        and dreaming of the combat zone.

Penelope, on a Diet

She's tried them all before
   and always failed, the war
      against her waistline more

than she can win alone,
   eating dinner on her own:
      some broth, a chicken bone

clad in a scrap of meat,
   a lettuce leaf replete
      with vinegar. Defeat

is just a Hershey's bar
   away, the gallon jar
      of peanut butter not far

enough beyond her reach.
   Some dieters beseech
      the gods for help. South Beach

and Atkins are divine,
   two deities thin as twine.
      Some women choose to dine

on nothing but the breeze,
   or no white foods, or string cheese,
      ham, and raspberries.

Some women pick protein
   instead of carbs, caffeine
      instead of lunch. They've seen

the opposite of fat
   is never thin – it's that
      solitude she can't combat,

no matter what she eats.
    She's still alone, still cheating
        on a fast she won't complete.

Another diet. There will
    be no way then to fill
        her stomach up, no pill

to kill the appetite.
    Alone, she will recite
        a prayer for each bite

of food. How good to digest
    cardboard, how very blessed
        that thirst can be suppressed.

At the Mall with Telemachus

First, he's pouting for
      French fries, a chocolate shake,
a toy from Burger King,
      and what a big mistake
if she doesn't give in –
      a fit of temper in
the food court, his legs a blur
      of speed, ten out of ten
on the tantrum scale,
      his voice an ambulance
at siren pitch, my god
      the screaming, the stridence
of his lungs, how long he holds
      each note, melismatic
as a mystic in a trance,
      or how his body's frantic
with its tick-tick-ticking,
      a toddler bomb about
to blow that cannot be
      defused although she shouts
at him to stop, just stop
      this nonsense now, and all
the mothers watching her
      embarrassment, appalled
but so relieved he's not
      their son, not theirs to spank
or bargain with or bribe,
      their little brat to yank
past Toys Я Us and drag
      away, while he grabs hold
of fistfuls of the greasy air
      and cannot be consoled.

Penelope Considers a New 'Do

The magazines declare don't ever cut
   your hair just after breaking up. So what
      if he's been absent nearly twenty years?
         Fact is: each day the loss feels new, the shears

still biting as the first time they'd been honed.
   Looks like he's never coming back. You've moaned
      for two decades about the shroud of bangs
         which veils your face, the way your ponytail hangs

down your back like a ragged piece of rope.
   Your follicles have given up all hope
      of *hair that moves*, of Farrah Fawcett's flip,
         Meg Ryan's shag, or anything so hip

as the pixie, the asymmetric bob.
   Go see the stylist-to-the-stars and sob
      your story out (that endless Trojan War,
         those gods). André has heard it all before.

He'll trim away dead ends so razor-fast –
   chop chop snip snip – you'll wonder why the past
      cannot be sliced so easily away
         or dyed a golden shade to hide the gray.

After Reading Tennyson

Matched with an agèd wife...

Some gall the poet has to call
   her old. The king is just as gray
and dull to boot, slouching in
   his La-Z-Boy, a can of Coors
perspiring in his hand. He snores.
   He burps. At times, to her chagrin,
she flinches when his fingers crawl
   across the chair toward her. Foreplay
is a myth – no kisses on her ear
   or the velvet creases of her neck.
Ulysses has no fight to warm
   her now. He's blunt as a rusted spear,
but she's still sharp, hardly a wreck,
   hardly a ship lost in the storm.

Odysseus, Sleeping

Penelope barely dozed,
      while he lay still
as a coiled rope
      or a windmill
waiting for the wind
      to spin its sails. Until
he shifted in a dream,
      she sometimes feared
that he had died
      already. His beard
was tarnish on his skin.
      She often peered
beneath the sheet to watch
      his fingers twitch
with lightning storms
      in miniature, bewitched
by how his body –
      like a sudden glitch
inside the circuitry
      – was both at rest
and perching on the edge
      of action, his chest
held half between two breaths.
      Who could have guessed
that soon he would become
      a motion made
perpetual, a strange
      machine afraid
to slow, to pause, to stop
      its turning blade?

In Penelope's Bedroom

A bottle of cologne still waits
   and waits for his return, evaporates
      to leave the passage of its scent
behind. She wonders where the fragrance went.

The right side of the bed must stay
   his side. She slips into her negligee,
      as if she's dressing still for him.
Perhaps her body cannot learn its grim

topography. She knows that life
   has dried her up. How terrible to be a wife
      made widow and yet still remain
married – what inaccessible terrain.

Whole regions that he used to kiss
   are now abandoned land. What does she miss
      the most? Without Odysseus
even her skin becomes extraneous,

a wrinkled, dusty map with few
   directions home. But long ago, trees grew
      in her, an orchard of perfume
that filled the farthest corners of the room.

What Odysseus Remembered

Each night, they grew together near the sink,
   his shoulder kissed by hers, and hers by his,
both rinsing the day from their skins.
   First he held the soap the way a man might make
a well of his palms, bucketing the white
   smoothness there. Next he passed the Ivory to her.
He felt her hands soft and open as an orchid,
   the bar now slippery, a wet stone.
She never let it slide onto the tiles.
   Soon he bent, as if about to drink,
then straightened to watch her in the mirror's gaze.
   And then she bent the thin stem of her neck –
no words, but water beaded on her lips,
   her face the pink of petals flushed with rain.

Instructions for Other Penelopes

spin what you can from his absence   a shroud
a crocheted throw in indigo and red

if mirrors crack cut jewels from the glass
comfort the muscular suitor with a kiss

comfort yourself   how long since you've been wound
or loosened from the loom   how long your hand

has worked the thread   fingered the filament
practice beauty as though it is an instrument

learn siren songs   forget the funeral hymn
pretend you are widow done with mourning

black will be the color of a tryst
and red will be a warning that you are past

the ashes of these twenty years   announce
your appetite   olives by the fistful   minced

garlic rubbed across a crust of bread
grapes giving up their stain   make an orchid

of your lips   a reckless garden of your skin
move   be still as marble   move again

call yourself mythology   converse
in rhyme in metaphor in Sapphic verse

how sweet to speak cinnamon and cloves
the taste of rosewater on your tongue   remove

your dress   the zipper opening like a V
or else imagine it   how easily

some layers are unpeeled while some remain
the pith and rind   the liquid heart   the stone

Penelope, Pluperfect

Before she had peppered
salt across her wrist,
had wrestled the heart
from its choke, had soaked
tea leaves for prophecy,
had seen a siren there,
had seen green sea, a god,
had sipped the afterward,
had tipped it down her throat,
had throttled it, had rapped
the egg to chip the shell,
had spooned the yolk from
its white bed, she licked
the liquid nova spilling gold.

Part Three

Oenophilia

Those months away from you, I teach myself
to cook with wine, admiring the change
a Beaujolais enjoys inside the pot,
its sly divestment of alcohol, slowly
from the heat, like a girl unbuttoning her blouse.
I'm indiscriminate. All reds will do
because you've never had a taste for white,
the frigid chardonnay or pinot gris
so chilled it makes the crystal goblet sweat.
You're loyal to the glass of claret light.
I'm talking warmth and things that need
to breathe before they're sipped. I mean
the old varietals, picked and stomped on,
a purpled bruise delicious for its pain,
the grape skin's shredded gauze. And so I plan
a week of meals that are a lesson in
desiring, like *Tristan und Isolde*,
where consummation never comes and booze
is an excuse for letting loose again,
again the bottle spilling liquid from
its open mouth, the green neck sticky there,
our tongues discovering the metal tannins
and something close to blood, but sweeter.

On the Erotics of Deployment

I'll build an altar
      to the tiny flecks fallen from his razor,

the pair of coveralls crumpled near the bed,
      the history of war he left unread.

The Goddess of Impermanence
      will be evicted from my home. In Her absence,

I will exhibit art
      composed of my vestigial parts,

my breasts the centerpiece
      to this display. I will be all of Greece

and Italy. I will forget about my skin
      and the awful need for friction,

how often I'm an empty plate.
      Or else, I won't forget but only tolerate

neglect. Some wives prefer
      to wait along the pier, green glitter

on their eyes, their bodies wrapped in scarlet.
      I'll try to be the harlot

that I want to be,
      Bathsheba gleaming on the balcony,

Susannah combing tangles from her hair.
      I will prepare

myself for him, a feast, a holy sacrifice.
      I'll be the fruit kept edible on ice.

Situational Awareness

These past few weeks I'm more than just aware
of where he is – I'm hypersensitive,
stretched thin as a length of wire, a hair-
trigger mechanism. Nothing can live
near me. I twitch each time the telephone
rings though the dark, so like a warning bell
I want to run from it, escape the Green Zone
of this house. Who said that war is hell?
Well, waiting can be worse. Show me a guy
shipped overseas, and I'll show you a wife
who sees disaster dropping from the sky.
The ambush always comes, her husband's life
a road of booby traps and blind spots made
to hide the rock, the shell, the thrown grenade.

Tendinitis

Stupid – the way the teacup, all at once,
weighs twenty pounds, trembling in its saucer
as though about to jump the edge, my wrist
and elbow like a pair of stunned strangers.

Turns out that living alone results in pain.
He used to haul the groceries from the car,
uncork the cabernet, screw lightbulbs in,
open the stubborn jar of marinara.

Twist, I tell my arm in the same voice
that I often said, *why don't you take
the garbage out*. How easy to dismiss
the constancy of limbs. I can barely skate

my hand into its mitten or tie my shoe.
The lesson here: lift fewer books or else
lift lighter ones. The lesson here: don't throw
a ball, don't drag a sweater from the shelf,

don't call the injury a metaphor
although it is, his absence sharp, hard
as a knob of bone, and my fingers,
clenching and unclenching what they cannot hold.

Stateside

If there is such
a thing as elasticity,
then we are stretched

nearly to the breaking.
The wait becomes my pulse,
come home come home.

Day eight, day nine, day ten,
day sixty-three.
When he comes home,

our miles increase,
the band pulled taut
between our separate points,

and we're released,
made slack again.
We almost don't belong

inside the same time zone,
much less this house.
He's *spouse*

instead of *lover,*
stateside instead of *overseas.*
I feel myself

withdrawing from his hand,
a touch I want
but barely understand.

VJ Day in Times Square

This is how distances begin – we two,
who hurry like a pair of travelers through
our home, each room a city block,
and often we are miles from talking.
I could wave at you from a kitchen chair
as though in a cafeteria. Upstairs
becomes its own municipality.
Sometimes there is the cordiality
of namelessness, the way one passerby
might intersect then hold another's eye,
smiling before the traffic light turns green.

But opening an art book, I've seen
us in that shot by Alfred Eisenstaedt.
Remember? A sailor holds a nurse, his hat
askew so that it seems about to fall,
forever tilting on his head. She's small,
although her body curves like steel, a bridge
suspended in that kiss. There's courage
in collision. Two pedestrians touch,
embracing in a photograph with such
quick ease it's hard to know why when we meet
we're cold as strangers passing on the street.

Surface Warfare

Our arguments move
across the surfaces
of things, smooth

flat areas where silence
floats for weeks.
The rule: whoever speaks

first loses. If he patrols
the living room,
then I control

our bed, an Atlantic
filled with my insomnia,
the quilts too thick

to wade through.
Some nights I think
drowning would be easier

and drink mouthfuls of salt.
No shallows here,
only the fathoms of marriage,

and we are anchored side
by side, the darkness wide,
percussive as a mine.

Winter Walk

after Enid Shomer

The leash loops
through your fingers
down to the dog's
soft neck. I watch
you tug the strap
as though you're fishing
him out of ice.
We pause on our path,
two trees he leans
away from, and wait
for the wind to drag
winter through his fur.
The park is frozen mud,
grooved and rutted
where many separate
bodies have stood.
I think how hard
all tethers can be –
the puppy straining
to snap his harness,
or a husband inclining
into a hotter season
each time he sees
another woman
walking by. I can't
stop imagining you
turned away from me
in bed, your back
bent like a branch
when you sleep:
how easily in dreams
you could follow
the scent of something
warm, shrug me off

for the yellow slant
of sun through maples,
and then the summer
breaking from its taut
restraint of rope.

Moving

That last night, we couldn't find our sheets
        but lay on furniture pads and barely slept,

the metal dolly in the corner of the room,
        a monster wheeled out from the gray closet

of childhood. The world was X-Acto knives
        and packing tape, boxes that spilled their secrets.

The world was a roll of bubble wrap that popped
        like a capgun going off, each wooden crate

a coffin for our valuables, a place
        to rest the porcelain vase on its side, flat

as a body. I can't say when I reached for you
        if we rustled like tissue paper, delicate

as shards, or if we slid our razored edges
        back and forth, until we split apart.

Navy Housing

On Jones Street every house is painted white,
each door is white, and every yard adheres
to certain rules: the grass at crew-cut height,
an apple blossom tree bent toward the sun,
a single bush trimmed squat and round and so
symmetrically it seems man-made. No one
can deviate from others in the row.
How easily I lose myself out here.
Even the dog can barely sniff his way
back from the park. Was it a left we took?
A right? Perhaps it's safer just to stay
indoors than go off course again. Oh, look –
another flag, another garden gnome,
another sign proclaiming HOME, SWEET HOME.

Bowl, in the Shape of a Bristol Boat

He carved the bowl for her, a hull so small
        it floated in the ocean of her palm,
rocked when she breathed, held still when she was still,

its body, purpleheart and maple,
        sanded and polished, sanded and rubbed until
the grain became a topographic map

by which to chart itself. The wooden bowl
        pushed forward, billowed a nonexistent sail.
No rudder guiding it, no mast or wheel.

The world was split between her hand and all
        the latitudes that lay beyond her hand –
a kitchen tabletop, a bookshelf filled

with Kant and Aristotle, a windowsill.
        He built the shell for her, as if to show
she was still water, and then the waterfall.

Intersection

At the corner of 31st and Utah Avenue,
even the streetlights seem to watch the stag
who must be lost, six blocks from Rock Creek Park
and stranded on the numbered streets. He stands
a yard from me, posed at the edge of grass
where geometric hedges meet the curb.
Already he has chewed green furrows in
the satin robe azaleas and made
a pattern of his hooves across the ground.

I do not move. His antlers are wrought iron,
his body still like a piece of lawn furniture
left out to rust. If I were braver – the kind
who writes often about the woods, not scared
of branches stripped in winter, the smell of musk –
I would open the blossom of my hand,
hold out its emptiness. And he would taste
the drying salt or touch his nose against
my wrist, lick the vein as if it were a stream.

Eastern Shore

Talking about distance is a way to close
the space. Consider the bridge that curves above
the Chesapeake, which when we mention it,
becomes a child's toy. Or that the Beltway
is not a contest of families wrapped in steel,
speeding toward collision, demanding it,
but just a road that circles on itself.
Remember when we touched at twenty-two,
so willingly aligned in one twin bed,
your spine pressed up against the wall and mine
about to break over the edge? These days,
we're greedy in our king, spread wide although
we barely scrape together in our sleep.
We're isolates with only water in between.
Closeness, you used to say, closing your arms
around me like a measurement of rope.
We fell asleep to Billie Holiday,
a long, sad looping of her voice that warned
not everyone is lucky in this world.
And I remember when you dressed for work,
how I hated watching as you tied each shoe,
the tight finality of laces cinched
in bows. It's been a while since I said
the buttons on your shirt reminded me
of afternoons and evenings spent in bed,
hours now indistinct as the facing shore,
our backs like metal arches, our words moving
from mouth to caverned mouth and mouth again,
the river of our bodies murmuring.

Shabbat Prayer, on the Occasion of War

beginning with a line from Siegfried Sassoon

A flare went up; the shining whiteness spread,
        as though it were a match bright enough
to light the room, but not so bright it snuffed
           the residue of darkness overhead.
There once was darkness signifying calm –
              our candles glowed
beside the window, the nights did not explode,
          or bullets ricochet, or firebombs
turn streets to ash. We drank a glass of wine.
        The night served as the complement to day,
like salt on something sweet. And, in this way,
          we tasted syrup mixed with brine.
And, in this way, we learned a prayer
        that joined the shadow with the shining flare.

ELYSE FENTON

CLAMOR

(2010)

CLAMOR

At times quiet, at others cacophonous, the poems of Elyse Fenton's *Clamor* turn a lyric lens on the language we use to talk about war and atrocity, and the irreconcilable rifts – between lover and beloved, word and thing – such work unearths. Originally published in the US – but not in the UK – in 2010, *Clamor* was the first book of poetry to win Britain's Dylan Thomas Prize.

Elyse Fenton is the author of two poetry collections, *Clamor* (Cleveland State University Press, 2010), first published in the UK in *Home Front*, and *Sweet Insurgent* (Saturnalia, 2017). She is the recipient of the Alice Fay di Castagnola Prize, the Cleveland State University First Book Award, the Pablo Neruda Award and the Bob Bush Memorial Award, and was selected as a New American Poet by the Poetry Society of America. Her poetry and prose have been published in *The New York Times, Best New Poets, American Poetry Review, The White Review, Pleiades* and *Prairie Schooner*, and have been featured on NPR's All Things Considered and PRI's *The World*. She has worked in the woods, on farms and in schools in Texas, New England, Mongolia, and the Pacific Northwest, and lives with her family in Portland, Oregon. *Clamor* was written when her husband was posted to Iraq as a US army medic.

http://www.elysefenton.com

FOREWORD

Elyse Fenton's poems are about something. That is, the poems in her book, *Clamor*, contain a discernible narrative and recognisable characters. The poems are about a woman waiting for a man to return from war and about what life is like for her when he returns. What makes the poems so compelling is the story she tells (both familiar and entirely new), the perfect forms she makes of her telling, and the space created between the story and the poems, which is an open field of speech, thought, desire and silence ('the saying, the not – '). There is a long history of women waiting for someone to return from war. Like many of these women, Fenton bides her time. She plants, she watches, she takes note. Carefully, carefully, she weaves her poems like Penelope at her loom. The making of poems is a way of marking time and of trying desperately to affect the passage of time.

Fenton's descriptions of her daily life and her imagined or overheard descriptions of events on the other front are hauntingly personal, moving, surprising. As a reader, I waited with Fenton for her beloved to return. I shamefully enjoyed the wait, the way waiting lends itself to a state of heightened attention and observation. I enjoyed the painful, precious suffering of longing. 'O make of me a human / camera to translate this restless flock,' writes Fenton whose poems are a kind of camera, one that we both look through and look at, for part of what the poems are about is the inability to translate experience into language but the absolute necessity of trying. 'I have to believe in more than *signifiers* – ' Fenton writes, 'that the world cannot be dismantled / by word alone. That language is not an uncoupling dance...' There is a real 'you' and an 'I' (sometimes called 'he' and 'she') and they love each other. Can love or language keep them safe? If not, is it then meaningless? ('It happened again just now. One word / Snagging like fabric on a barbed fence.') No. The poems do not make the war end, do not bring the 'he' home sooner, do not erase the war from anything even when he does return.

But the words do matter; the word, any word, from or about the beloved matters so very much. The poems are a record of Fenton's fidelity both to her love and to language – no matter how difficult things get she is there with eyes and ears and heart open. The care and consciousness of Fenton's poems – lines, language, sound – is almost superstitious in its intentionality, but is never distracting or upstaging. Fenton is a poet with a story to tell; a poet finding the perfect forms to tell her tale. For example, when deployment ends the poems assume the shape of prose and even without line-breaks, they are crushingly beautiful, almost intolerably beautiful. The poems create intimacy even as they are always (even after his return) describing a kind of absence. The poems create a space where the poet and her beloved are together. Over and over but each time in new and surprising ways, Fenton brings the two fronts (the war and the homefront) together. She elides her present into that of the absent lover's present. In one poem her walls are 'flower-mortared', and the leaf she presses into her wrist is the dog-tag that the soldier removes from a dead body.

There is both shame and pleasure in the poet's love of language, in the language of engagement, of war, of death, of destruction, but such care and attention on Fenton's part is necessary, admirable, for it is through the examination of the language of deployment and civilian life that readers such as myself, who wait for no specific solider to return and have only an abstract sense of war's ravages, can begin to *feel* the war.

Fenton's poems allow the war to be a metaphor for life, for waiting, for separation, for the way in which all couples are always separated in and by their distinct points of view and independent experiences. The poems also insist on specificity and are always about *this* war and *this* time, this 'I' and this 'he'.

When I read *Clamor* I cried. When I read it again, I cried earlier and harder and longer. It is not often that a book of poems has this effect on me. I wanted to keep reading, to know what would happen and how. And, more than that, I wanted to keep hearing Fenton's voice, to savor her careful observations of the sun, the garden, bodies, longing, absence, presence – to marvel at her deft lines, to shiver as she brought the war home for me.

RACHEL ZUCKER

CLAMOR

For P. –

I want to gather you up
into a book whose pages clink

like bone cockles gaveled smooth
in the blood-wash of unimagined shore –

clamor –

1. *a: A noisy shouting b: A loud continuous noise*
2. *Insistent public expression (as of support or protest)*
3. *SILENCE*

Gratitude

Wreckage was still smoldering on the airport road
when they delivered the soldier – *beyond recognition,*

seeing God's hands in the medevac's spun rotors –
to the station's gravel landing pad. By the time you arrived

there were already hands fluttering white flags of gauze
against the ruptured scaffolding of ribs, the glistening skull, and no skin

left untended, so you were the one to sink the rubber catheter tube.
When you tell me this over the phone hours later I can hear rotors

scalping the tarmac-gray sky, the burdenless lift of your voice.
And I love you more for holding the last good flesh

of that soldier's cock in your hands, for startling his warm blood
back to life. Listen. I know the way the struck chord begins

to shudder, fierce heat rising into the skin of my own
sensate palms. That moment just before we think

the end will never come and then
the moment when it does.

I.

The Beginning

January, Boston. She held his first letter back
from the new front in her hands. Outside, light

and snow clung to the train windows like the paper
edges of a hive crushed in. Later she would remember

otherwise; not the long rows of parking spots
tunneled from snowbanks and marked

with plastic lawn chairs like tombstones
for the unprepared or the pigeons on Comm Ave

mistaking salt for crumbs. Not the neon swarm
of flakes or the first few notes of grief

waiting to unfold. Only that she looked up
from the page – *Only now am I afraid to die* –

to feel the desperate clamor of a train
jerking roughshod through its gears,

the car's slow rocking-in-its-tracks
like the heart's smallest engine

                    just beginning to seize –

Love in Wartime (I)

Because there are seven thousand miles
of earth & sky between us. Because

these lines are made of wind & fired
particles. Because at any moment the hard dust
beneath your feet could breach like a cleft
in meaning, could erupt into a sifting
cloud of brick & metal-riven bone

I have to believe in more than *signifiers* –

that the world cannot be dismantled
by the word alone. That language is not
an uncoupling dance or the sparkless grinding
of meaning's worn flint, a caravan of phosphorus
tails burning up the breathable air.

When I say *you* I have to mean
not some signified presence, not
the striking of the same spent tinder

but your mouth & its live wetness, your tongue
& its intimate knowledge of flesh.

Word from the Front

His voice over the wind-strafed line
                 drops its familiar tone to answer,
Yes, we did a corkscrew landing down
   into the lit-up city, and I'm nodding

on my end, a little pleased by my own
                 insider's knowledge of the way
planes avert danger by spiraling
   deep into the coned center of sky

deemed safe, and I can't help but savor
                 the sound of the word – the tracer round
of its pronunciation – and the image –
   a plane *corkscrewing*

down into the verdant green
                 neck of Baghdad's bottle-glass night
so I don't yet register the casual solemnity
   of newscaster banter

falling like spent shells
                 from both our mouths, nor am I
startled by the feigned evenness
   in my lover's tone, the way

he wrests the brief quaver
                 from his voice like a pilot
pulling hard out of an engineless
   plummet, but only at the last minute

and with the cratered ground
                 terrifying, in sight –

Notes on Atrocity (Baghdad Aid Station)

Mid-conversation someone comes
looking for body bags. Medic,

I can hear you rummaging
the shelves, know the small fury

of your hands and the way
they used to settle, palms sinking

heavy bodies into mine. Outside
on my end, frost whittles the grass

to shards, the pear tree breathes
beneath a shroud of ice. When your voice

drifts above the shifted boxes, overheard,
it's washed in a tenderness I know

I'm not supposed to hear. As if
this were not the work of shrapnel –

not the body's wet rending, flesh
reduced to matter – but the litany

of an old field guide, the names
of wildflowers spoken out loud:

ischium, basal ganglia, myelin-
sheathed endings. Names for parts.

For all our flowering parts.

After the Blast

It happened again just now. One word
snagging like fabric on a barbed fence.

Concertina wire. You said: *I didn't see the body
hung on concertina wire.* This was after the blast.

After you stood in the divot, both feet
in the dust's new mouth and found no one alive.

Just out of the shower, I imagine
a flake of soap crusting your dark jaw, the phone

a cradle for your bare cheek.
I should say: *love.* I should say: *go on.*

But I'm stuck on *concertina* –
the accordion's deep inner coils, bellows,

lungful of air contracting like a body caught
in the agony of climax. Graceless

before the ballooning rush
of air or sound. That battering release.

Aubade, Iraq

Sulfur-mouthed nightcrier, rooftop
harbinger, bringer of the gut-shot

dawn – what I would do to keep you
at rifle's reach, stifle you, drown you

in the Tigris' muck and swill, touch you
aflame on its kerosene spine.

I could wait out artillery skitter, crater-
blast, stay here long into next empire

dreaming fingers and the Fertile Crescent
of thighs – if not for your voice

risen like Babel's ghost from the ruined fortress,
ash-haired rider come to tongue open

dawn's torturous eye –

The Riots in Bangalore

An icon of South Indian cinema and star of more than 200 films, Raj Kumar died on Wednesday, sparking widespread violence as distraught fans torched buses and ripped scaffolding in the country's hi-tech hub.

REUTERS

Morning in April, the war still on, sun silting the kitchen
like coffee grounds in the sink. In yesterday's *Times*

mourners in India ripped doors from hinges, smashed

loose shutters. Like the ancient Rites of Spring –
steer roasts in the budding groves, lions waiting to be fed –

the pageantry of death so close to bliss. The street's all aftermath:

torched cars, trampled grass. The day hoisted by its shoulders
and carried away. After all these months, I've come to expect

nothing less of despair. A hero dies and why not

take to the streets, join the cherry trees rallying into bloom?
Death so close you can reach out and tear a board

from the casket, taste the bitter singe of rubber in the air.

And why not follow the ambulance like Orpheus's keening
head down the river of bodies, add another voice to the severed

song? Even now, as grief threatens to strip the world to its naked

scaffolding – the war entering a third year, you still nine months
from home – blossoms swarm my window and the sun

impulsively flashes, bare flesh beneath a shredded veil.

The First Canto

I know you've waited for this call all day, felt the tank's
panes rattle twice from the nearest shell, air shuddering

like talus underfoot. Ninety-eight degrees in Baghdad
and you say the heat hasn't yet arrived, though I can feel it, the
    armored

weight of days, your voice spreading like crescents of sweat
beneath each fold of cloth. Today I don't ask about the war, your
    afternoon

shredding envelopes into the burn barrel, if any bodies came in.
Instead, I want to tell you about the First Canto, dark woods, a trail

turned first to thicket and then to shale. A man brought to the edge
of the cindery lip to peer in. Even Dante had a choice: to ascend

the sunny mantle of light or take the fast slope down, to flee
the wolf approaching, his own fear. There was no catch

but the cold lake growing in his heart, small terror
like the plash of an oar loosened from its hold. He didn't wait

to see the wolf's gray mange, its scurvied hide, the broken teeth
betraying hunger for the sun. He chose first to descend, and you –

you chose the war. Seventeen months now and you're a shade
leaning into the soot-grimed mouth of the oil drum, whip of sparks

lashing your hands, the book I sent you, unread, at your feet.

The War Bride Waits

Sometimes it's like the last scene in a Western where only the
    horses are left
grazing an apocalypsed field. There they are, stranded amid
    crabgrass in the blessing

of their own bulky bodies, having survived the long ride, having
    missed
the bullets of outlaws or the tragic implications of fate, quietly
    bathed in a gold light

meant to signify the dawning *END*. There's always a fade-out, the
    rising
bird-on-a-bent-wing scrawl of names meaning we should expect
    nothing more,

no last plot twist, no surprise rock-fall, no lover waiting off-screen
    to turn up
for the hero's dream of death. This is the moment the dead are
    mercifully allowed

to stay dead, the moment in the dull celluloid flicker when the
    last horse caught
in the narrowing lens lifts its bent neck expectantly and looks
    around.

Planting, Hayhurst Farm

A week since the last bombing
brought you to your knees, since

the day you spent shoveling
human remains into a body bag

marked for home. I don't know
what to say. Neither of us has slept.

But today, planting peppers
on a farm in Oregon nowhere near

the war, I found myself mid-way
down a row, on all fours, hands

breaking open the rocky clods
coaxing the flimsy necks to stand.

It felt like an exercise
in good faith – my fingers

blindly plunging, a brief tenderness
exacted on every stalk.

Some didn't make it through
our rough caging, some will never

bear fruit. I don't know if this
is even meant as consolation

but I want to tell you just how easy
it became to plant the thin bodies

in the ground, to mound up
that dense soil and move on.

Love in Wartime (II)

Outside, on the rocks
>   the Japanese maples thrash
>   their wind-wracked limbs.

The clamor of branches, lines
>   of worshippers stampeding a mosque;

your gloved soldier's hands feeding out
>   bloodied reams of gauze.

>   *Holy, holy, holy:*

the violence of those leaves, their purple,
>   arterial sheen.

I want to say
is what I keep saying, over and again.

It goes on like this.

The wind, the saying, the not –

Public Mourning (Flag Installation)

One-hundred-sixty-six thousand flags
sodding the lawn like the hand-flung crumple
of scrap on the Liberation Day street. Ticker-
taped. Wired down into unfreeze, ground-
swell, into a harvest of heave and worm.

One-hundred-sixty-six thousand paper
carapaces like the eyelids of the living
sprung forth with all the nubbled blindness
of the newly dead. O make of me a human
camera to translate this restless flock.

Friendly Fire

I

Caught between gunner and gunner,
slough and sand bank, clamor and clamor.

Pill and bitter pill.

II

Also called *fratricide*. As if
uniforms or tanks made kin, brothered-in-

Cain rising from dune-heather
like tracer smoke, ultimatum.

Abel tripping through the seam-rent dawn
into the eye of the scope.

Above the thornbelt, sky'd shrapnel, God's own eyes
waiting to see what would be done.

III

As if the flames were meant alone to warm.

Cookfire, hearth, hot rocks for bread.
The lit faces of ecstatics. A joyful flickering.

IV

Slender-tongued tracer arc. Sweet talker.

Long-time lover throwing wide her arms
to shield you. Friendly fire, sulfur-choked

passion – nothing of betrayal sparking
her open and tendered mouth.

Metal Sandwich

In the dream-logic of last night's two separate dreams
I ate metal in a doughy bun and then watched my molars
crumble and split lengthwise in the next. *Rotten junk,*
the dream doctor said and tendered a metal fist before
I woke to a morning full of consequence and holes.

Ballistic

The article quoted the private as saying
they'd been *thinking with their guns again*

by way of explanation. The context doesn't matter;
the soldiers were expected to survive. It's not hard

to imagine the brain's ballistics, tamped neurons,

a bullet throttled from bore to breech. Take the way
I understood last night's dream. One crumbling tooth

as the ghost pain of a limb my body had become –
and then you gone when I dreamed I woke and gone still

for the real waking, morning's paralysis of sun.

What strange misfire, stutter in the synaptic gap,
though it could be much worse: all coordinates

misaligned or lost, the real bullet fished finally
from the unconscious sergeant's skull

and strung around his waiting lover's neck.

For L., in Baghdad

A fuselage of crows has beggared
the January seed. They lurch from limbs

then upstart, near the ground. Iron marrow,
rust. What happened to the will to fly?

Here, it's record-breaking cold. A breaking
cold that never breaks.

Do me a favor, L. Stay put. Stay close
to earth. The days are nose-diving

to an end. Keep a record of the bodies there
and I will keep a tally here of mine.

Refusing Beatrice

Dante needed a whole committee–
Beatrice, Lucy, Virgil– to guide him
                                    down and back, even though hell

was a known descent, a matter of pages, a book
ending in certainty with a hero seeing stars.

        You've got no itinerary. Just an armored car
                to ferry you down the graveled airport road, a Chinook

                gut-deep in the green swill waiting to dislodge.

Maybe it's time to stop comparing –
I could never be Beatrice, couldn't harbor such good faith.

        And I won't be there in the Tigris basin to watch
                heat flake cinders of paint from the Chinook's body
                                        like a rug shook out

        or see it hasten to the sky's surface
                                    like an untethered corpse –

My curse or gift is blindness;
                I've never read this story before.

        And if the updraft's whirlwind
                doesn't make the sniper miss, if your helicopter lifts

                from Baghdad as doomed as the Chaldean sun,

        I won't be there to see the wreckage
                or papery flames, the falling arsenal of stars –

Love in Wartime (III)

The teacher wanted a clearer starting place

A map or else a mapping on –
Towns, green hills, a common vein of road.

Newspapers that spoke overtly
or else never spoke of war.

But in the poem's road
there was always something burning.

Petrol blue-smoked the borders
and no one was allowed out or in.

Somewhere a clot of tarmac singed
brightly like light through scrubby trees

and it was impossible to step from the median
without mouthing

minefield, lodestar, beautiful amputee –

Charon

Before the Acheron, before the fret and fester
of oars in the stream, before days that mounted
like carcasses stripped from shades and the words
for everything sloughed like side-meat
from water-softened bone –

There was *sun* and *slough*.
There was *shin-deep in the quick waters*
and places where the mayflies' wing-drag
filigreed the air, where my own hook-flash
wracked the mud skinned-surface

and a hundred violent mouths rose up to feed.

For Radha, Two Days Old

It's winter and the war's still on.

Ice cauls our windows, snow
paraffins the trees.

No silage, petrol, no forethought
can save us from this cold,

nor spring return to us
our dead.

Just days ago, slash smoldered
on the coast road.

Hold on, tiny faith, warm coal.
Radha, let us touch your face,

thaw our fingers on your kindled skull,
trace the kerf of your open mouth.

Abide us.

The fields are stubble
where the drip-torch slurred.

We have nothing left to burn.

Aftermath

His job was not to salvage
but to bundle the clothes – trash bags full of uniforms
Rorschached in blood, boot-tips testing toed-thin plastic
like cheekbones testing skin, loose tongues in search
of a foot or a name –
                              and then carry it all out
to the incinerator and wait until new smoke hoisted
            the black flag of daybreak that would billow and rise and fade.

Late February (Persephone)

In the front yard I loosen sod,
return the lawn to earth and seed,
   listen for the twang of the spade-head
      channeling the chthonic ground.

   Meanwhile the earth stands still.
The sun's ball-bearing cools, gaskets
   out of time and in the limbs of trees
      the water-thinned sap unspools.

   This month extends its promise of rain and rain-
greased boughs but instead of amends I make
   myself a bulb in a worm-hole, mouth-piece
      for the spade-mouthed dead.

What We Hold, We Hold at Bay

Along the hedge along the rail
lilacs hold purple bouquets of rain

at eye-level, leveling the dewy
buckets of their eyes at mine

so passing the next flower-mortared
wall I swipe a slice of leaf and press

its lacquered numerals to my wrist
to let its oaky face-plate register my pulse.

Palm-reader, I read a patchy guess-
work and hold the leaf the way

I think you must have held
a dog-tag slipped from around the collar

of the dead before you zipped the soldier
into his leafy cask –

                        but I can't decipher a name

from any of these veins or read
the engrafted petals of this Braille

and without a chain to save it on
I can only lift it to the record of my lips:

leaf-metal burnished with the breath
of rain, on which I try to find your breath –

Clamor

Staking fencing along the border of the spring
garden I want suddenly to say something about
this word that means sound and soundlessness
at once. The deafening metal of my hammer strikes
wood, a tuning fork tuning my ears to a register
I'm too deaf to understand. Across the yard

each petal dithers from the far pear one white
cheek at a time like one blade of snow into
the next until the yard looks like the sound
of a television screen tuned last night to late-
night static. White as a page or a field where
I often go to find the promise of evidence of you

or your unit's safe return. But instead of foot-
prints in the frosted static there's only late-
turned-early news and the newest image of a war
that can't be finished or won. And because last
night I turned away from the television's promise
of you I'm still away. I've staked myself

deep to the unrung ground, hammer humming
in my hand, the screen's aborted stop-time still
turning over in my head: a white twist of rag
pinned in the bloody center of a civilian's chest,
a sign we know just enough to know it means
surrender, there in the place a falling petal's heart would be.

II.

Deployment Ends

November morning. Dusky pellicle of frost on the ground. When his plane finally touched down, when he imagined her pocketed hands, her pacing in the terminal he thought he would have to turn away. There was too much harm in the world for this small province of safety to go acknowledged. When he walked down the long terminal he swung his hands. As if he had no baggage to remind him of the way.

After the War

They lived like revenants, just outside the gate. He was The Returned. She was the one who propped the storm door to watch the empty street. The first lesson was simple: learn the name of a blessing and then speak it within earshot of the other. At first she could only think, *Meekness*. January's thigh-shriveled light or the muteness, even, of birds. The way a whole tree's-worth of crows enacted Quiet-Homage-to-Despair and not one of them ever startled at the Apaches throttling overhead.

At some point she forgot to think of a blessing. Even the days started to pass. And then this morning when she was standing in the doorway she saw the sun throw its jacket across the top of the barbed perimeter fence – like an escapee – so that nothing would catch or tear. The next blessing would have to be forgiveness and for a whole day she believed it would last.

By Omission

I didn't know I was empty-holstered, her husband was saying, *until after we'd passed the gate*. They were at the kitchen table with the neighbors and everyone but her was back from war. The light outside was dusk, a rag full of holes, an hourglass leaking salt. A neighbor flipped a bottle cap in his hand. She'd heard about the bodies, his bagging of the dead, how to pull a dogtag from its chain. But not this detail before. *How do you forget your gun?* she asked. She was imagining the empty cradle where he must have put his hand. Tenderness or refusal, thoughtlessness, surprise or dread. Outside, the dusk was losing. A glass sang out against the table's edge and when he said nothing she knew every silence was a lie he couldn't tell.

Commerce

There wasn't enough forgiveness to go around. Dogs led themselves around the block. At the pawn shop down the street you could buy anything, even someone else's false teeth. The whole day it rained and then was sunny and then it rained some more. She was sitting at her desk reading a book. When she looked a word up in the dictionary, she remembered one from a dream. It was just like that, two for the price of one, and then, action following word: how she pulled the plug from the wall and *wound* the cable up; how when he came back into the room in his uniform, the *wound* opened some more. Each meaning haunted by the next. By then it was growing dark and the whole western sky was gold pried from a stranger's mouth. There are smaller prices for having survived.

Complicity

She's halfway through the line at the store when she overhears the clerk say, *My husband? He's off at war.* The clerk leans both hands on the counter like an old grandmother in some country of ground-freeze and broken glass. At the register they're two women across a plastic counter. Do they want to tell each other everything they know about the war? Some complicities she's never felt. In the other country, women gum seeds in their mouths, let the empty shells speak for themselves. On the counter, the paper receipt curls against itself. She reaches for spilled coins and feels a tongue push back against her teeth.

Endurance

I used to stand in doorways and know
there was no human way to go on or through –

Mercy

I had a friend who broke his neck in a rugby game. One straight fracture right at the base, only he didn't know it and neither did we. He went home that night in pain and didn't come out to the bar. When we called the next morning he'd already driven himself to the hospital where they'd guided him into a C-collar and bolted a metal halo to his skull.

I remembered him just now when I ran my hand along your scalp, the divot where a surgeon's scalpel dove. Even before you left for war, you had these scars to show. Bone fused just at the brink. I think I envy your surgeon his hands, the deftness of a bone-saw sunk from skull to blade guard, their knowledge that mercy's sole attendant is pain.

I don't believe in any higher power, my friend was saying the time I saw him next. *But if I had had to turn my head at any point along the way, I would be dead.* For every word he spoke, the halo's shadow trembled, lightening his darkened face.

Bridge

One fall we humped logs up to a bridge site near Wildcat, bush-whacked a shortcut the entire way. Each time we dropped lumber at the site we pried up bridge spikes and shouldered chunks of the rotten stringers for the trip down. For three days it went on like that, shouldering and un-shouldering loads, mashing ferns into duff, tearing briars and their rusty cables from our hair. Late October and the season was about to unleash a killing cold. Our work was supposed to be done. We beat the snow until the new bridge had to go up. I remember nothing of that process. Only flakes beginning to thicken on our last trip down, that final, stricken weightlessness like submission or the moment I realised you'd survived the war though the war would never be won.

Married

In a backyard tent I told you the story of Guy Waterman's ghost.
How, climbing past Little Haystack, the wind took up the dirt
into his form and then was gone. There was the sound of rockslide
but not a single stone had moved. You told me about a child who
pressed herself into the attic window while the rest of her body
burned. On the upper lining of our tent was a skin of breath or
early dew. And after making love, we made of our returning bodies
a smoky pane so that the dead could see us too.

III.

Through a round aperture I saw appear
Some of the beautiful things that Heaven bears,
Where we came forth, and once more saw the stars.

Inferno, Canto XXXIV

Veteran's Day

Today the wind's predictable, flowering the brown lawn
with the dead gloved thumbs of leaves like a rusted

poppy-strafed field.   *Live Oak*

I remember hearing for the first time long before Texas –
without knowing taxonomy or that living

basketry of limbs – and thinking in what desolate
place is this title not redundant?

Live Oak, quercus virginiana. And now I see it's a name
befitting itself and I want to rename everything this morning:

Live Low Cumulus   Live Rain-Sheened street   Live Sun

bone-sawing through a gap in the leaves. And earlier, Live
Flesh of your flesh when I slipped my hand beneath your shirt

and felt the impatient work of your working heart
from beneath an unwreathed cenotaph. Your ribs.

Mesquite

All I want above my grave is a mesquite tree
  Frank Dobie said, so all morning on your stoop

outside the base's barbed perimeter fence, I've been reading
  mesquite as testament to readiness

and thirst, leaves chittering above hardpan and roots
  displacing everything that came before

What memorial: sweet starch of survival
  in the bark, needles re-threading the shaggy limbs.

And now, asleep on the couch in your desert
  camo, boot tips splayed like dead cactus flowers,

your body's a spiny thorn and there are shovel-blunt
  consequences for your return. Alkaline veins

in the earth, raptors stealing sun or the metal
  husks of shells and no chance

for a quick or catastrophic death. Sleep, my love,
  my Hopeless Returned. Leaf out

into another body: the body no waking moment
  will allow you to become –

Persephone as Model for the Soldier, Returned

Imagine villagers outside Avernus leaving
their stoves ajar, tongues guttering the grates,

to see what flame you'd remake your body by.

Spring, and with a villager's hands I crack
black rot from shells, hedge old bets and push the beans

down into unfreezing muck. Re-read
the almanac's advice on how to overwinter well

and wait.

*

Waiting, I watched forsythia come alive
between the fence's broken slats.

And when I looked up, a bottle rolled, wind-
gust down the street.

Was it like that?

Simply obeying a season?
February's slow-becoming Spring?

*

Beneath the Spring, tectonic plates that never
quit. A voice saying *Don't forget!* even as

it was starting to break up.
On the surface, snow's crackle, static.

A puddle of grackles beak-deep in mud.
One long tremor after another

and the birds still jawing and diving
as if trying to get through.

*

Even as we made it through, planting
seeds in earthen pots, in rows, in

the overbearing ground, we took
your silence for the slow speech of thaw.

How could we have known a pit
stuck like a bloody molar in your mouth?

The thing that, trying and trying–
        you can never spit out–

*

Split root, dual stranger. Beloved.

Please tell me only your feet remember
what the earth beneath the earth was like.

Your Plane Arrives from Iraq for the Last Time

Texas overcast. The road toward post
needle-pricked in brake lights, start-
and-stop of the heart's four chambers

involuntarily bound. And once more
the sky's feathered jet-stream, and once
more, the dirge and caesura of rotors

and once more the slow Morse of the plane's
body descending. And at the end
of the longest sentence I've ever known

your face in the window's fogged aperture:
stranded noun, Rorschach of stars. *Beautiful thing.*

Garden

No gardener, you watch from the deck
as I scrape weedy belts from the green
waists of spinach and kale. May evening

and the sun's bayoneted on a paintless post
across the yard – enough to blind us with –
so when I look up from the slatey loam I look

East and catch you squinting into the ambered
blood of the Western sky, a glassy shoot of bottle-
light sprouted from your Returning Soldier's hands.

After Discussing Your Original Reasons for Enlisting

I dream we're raccoon traders hustling punctuation-
sized babykins out of their thatch-box rookeries – they're
more like chickens in the cellular dreamlight – and our BB
guns are smokeless invocations. When the cops come at full
tilt in a golf cart I can only stand and gawk at the questions
forming in the question-riddled air while you, my heartthrob
war hero minus the hero, stand mute as a comma, one insistent
newborn mewling in the crook of each hesitant arm.

Poem without Throat or Song

Morning finds me over-
steeped   a garden unturned

unshirred clod thieved
from frost's last catacomb

a dew-wrecked coffer   a dormant
lantern   a muted cocoon

a guttering guildering

a guilting thing –

Conversation

We're disparate as men counting
miles across an ocean renamed home,
you and I and the heart's joists that keep
the roof from warping under broken

pipes and wind. *No one marries during war*
I'm told and yet I'm married to the thought
of you returning home to marry me
to my former self. The war is everywhere

at once. Each eggplant that I pick
is ripe and sun-dark in its own inviolable
skin. Except there is no inviolable anything
and you've been home now for a year.

In the Fourth Year of War (Killeen, TX)

Here, morning means another
dogged black wing of light snagged

like a wind-gust bag plastered
to the perimeter fence;

you gone before crow-squawk wakes
the standing legion of trees.

What the trees forgive I have
tried as well: dawn's doilied prayer

scarf lifted from their armored
limbs before any prayer's

been said; or the hasped voices
of crows, their rotor-edged nay-

saying like the constant drone
of planes. *Come back O Come Back.*

Every morning test flights test
my old resolve to stay close

to earth. Call it failure or
respite, call it gravity's

portrait of grace. Still, there's no
disputing the stuttered flight

of light or crows from one branch
to the gnarled next. They lift

and drop and snag like notes
along the heart's barbed chord. A song.

Commission

In the poem you asked me for we're driving
west – though we never have before – toward
the western sun and each mile gained we slough

a bit of self. By the time we hit the coastal
shacks we're cliff-side and eroded bare. Or else
eroded new. With what measured mercy I can proffer

you I draw a fishing boat's fresh clutch of gulls
to swoon in circles overhead and hinge my hands
into the razor clam's promise of sand or sandy flesh.

North Coast

I

All evening the best-of-the-season sun's been faking
resurrection, wandering an astral boast above our sun-

burnt heads while we probe the shore's supply
of tide-worn stones for surface travel on a glazier's bay.

Low tide unscrolls a surfy bricolage of shell
and carapace and kelp and finally we're prepared to see

whatever else we stand to lose. Civilian at last
you squint into the dazzling proof of sun, warm stone

in your stone-warmed hands and say, *I've never seen a day
last through itself like this*, then stand and chuck the stone
                                        into the seamless bay.

II

The sea lifts its mapmaker's hands
to the silty bay edge, drafting a border
in briny scrawls the squirts and crabs

ignore. This close to North the sun
protracts an angle heretofore unknown

as all things I didn't know before
you returned from war. Now

you drowse across a splintered sea-
drift log, arms loosened at their sockets
like the unbuckled carapace of crab

beaked belly-up by a marauding gull:
that winning Portrait of a Fallen Hero pose.

Near sleep too, I build a driftwood
raft with woody rays of sun to drift us

out past tide break so that I might shoot
a bull-kelp bearing in sixty-four directions
and sketch out the farthest skein of map

the tide's – just now – withdrawn.

The Dreams

O The Dreams are back, The Dreams won't let me
        alone, The Dreams have gatekeepers
in trench coats woven from tyre shavings and thorn

and whenever I hasten toward the sleep of the sleep-
        bludgeoned, the boulder placid in a talus-field of sleep
the gatekeepers shake the rattlesnake bushes that pillow

my head and club the cracked parchment of my feet.
        O The Dreams are bitter, are creosote and char and can't
let me forget their dozen names. The Dream of Death or Dis-

appointment, the Dream of the Inscrutable with its hot
        disks tattooed like your name into flesh, stripped
guy-lines to hoist the crow-sorrowed horizon aloft.

Coffee

Because the brew I'm steeping sees me mid-page
through a book of poems about the war I have to
choose whether to leave this page's body for grinds
that burble through the coffee press like the body
of the early-winter earth that called me to attention
with its empty-handed mix of mud and snow the day
I deemed you *Morning Wisp of Dew* zeroing like steam
from the top of my daily mug – or else sit through
these kettle-thralls until they wake you from the war
into our room nearby where the sheets are pages
I've torn back in search of morning's grinds, and you.

Days and Nights of Your Return

Sometimes it's darkness the heart's engine
lifts the body into. Like the test flights

of aircraft crowning the night's steady tar

or thought's crook-necked bird nestled
unspoken in the brain's loose scree.

As if there were something preternatural

about the rise of any form into a visible
space – the blind whir of rotors

bearing the plane's body into foggy view

or the acetylene shock of the skin's
presence becoming known–

From a separate darkness we number

the days, watch our bodies' stricken falling
from a distance, each feather of longing

skiffed off a turning wing.

Infidelity

When you were in Iraq I dreamed you
dead, dormant, shanked stone

in a winter well, verb-less object
sunk haft-deep through the navel

of each waking sentence. I dreamed
myself shipwreck, rent timbers

on a tidal bed, woke to morning's cold
mast of breath canted wide as a searchlight

for the drowned. Dreamed my crumbling
teeth bloomed shrapnel'd bone light

bricks mortared into a broken
kingdom of sleep where I found you

dream-sift, rubbled, nowhere.
Forgive me, love, this last

infidelity: I never dreamed you whole.

Roll Call

No matter the details. It always ends
at the sweat-salt metal of your un-
answered name. Twenty-one triggers
and twelve-hundred bit-down tongues.

Last clamor of the swan-beaked rifle.
Last unmuzzled throatful of air.

LIST OF ABBREVIATIONS

AWOL: Absent without leave.

BB gun: Air gun which fires spherical projectiles.

BFPO: British Forces Post Office.

CIC: Combat Information Center (US Navy), i.e. the Operations Room or Action Information Centre (British Navy).

GPMG: General-purpose machine gun.

MOD: Ministry of Defence.

R & R: Rest and recuperation (or relaxation).

RTMC: Reserves Training and Mobilisation Centre.

INDEX OF TITLES